FRIED FISH AND PHYLACTERIES

A glimpse of being Jewish in England

Dennis Hardy

First published 2021

© Dennis Hardy 2021

Enquiries concerning these terms should be addressed to

Blue Gecko Books

bluegeckobooks@ymail.com
www.bluegeckobooks.com

ISBN:978-0-9575685-2-5

Design and formatting by Barbara Velasco (Papel+Papel Creative)

Cover Photograph and Design © Jane Woolfenden

Tree logo by Genzi @ istock

To my brother Robin

and

to the memory of our sister Jill (1948-2021)

Fried fish binds Anglo-Jewry more
than all the lip-professions of unity
(Israel Zangwill, Children of the Ghetto)

... this sceptr'd isle,
This other Eden, demi-paradise;
This precious stone set in the silver sea...
This blessed plot, this earth, this realm, this England
(John of Gaunt, in Shakespeare, Richard II, II i)

And may he live in Manchester
(Words added in Aleppo to the traditional
circumcision blessing for an infant son)

Next year in Jerusalem
(A wish expressed at the end of
the annual Passover service)

Contents

Foreword

Anti-Semitism is rearing its ugly head again. Maybe it never went away. One had always hoped that the Second World War would have been a turning point, a catharsis to clear the poison that had lingered in the body for too long. But that was not to be; such optimism was ill-founded. Recent incidents in Europe and America, not to mention in the Jewish homeland that won international approval at the time of its creation in 1948, are sufficient to warn that the world cannot sit idly by.

If it is not to spread, the great institutions of government – international as well as national – have a responsibility to act. Anti-Semitism is an offence to common decency and an enemy of human rights. Can the reasons for its continuing presence be rooted out once and for all? Why do Jews continue to be the target for so much abuse? What can be done to change fundamental attitudes that are so antagonistic? How can we lay foundations for a less fractious future? These are big questions and cannot be left simply to official bodies to answer. Ordinary Jews, going about their everyday business, can play their own part. Indeed, one might argue that this is where it should all start: in families and schools, in communities and cultural activities.

This homespun book is a modest contribution towards healing old wounds. It differs from great declarations and weighty reports in two ways: it draws on the stories of related families who have lived in England for generations, and it uses history to chip away at some of the big questions.

How did the project arise? Spontaneously, different family members decided it was time to find out more about our various ancestors. Digital records and online searches make this kind of enquiry easier to manage than it might once have been. But 'easy' is not the word to use in trying to follow the intricate twists and turns of individuals in the past, all making history in their own way. In looking for fragments of evidence, we have made frequent contact with each other, sharing information and helping to fill in vexatious knowledge gaps.

I am simply the scribe, drawing on the hard work and curiosity of others, and trying to put together a narrative to describe what has been found.

No less, I have attempted to set the individual stories in context, in an attempt to give them more meaning. Above all, I have seen this as an exploration of 'Jewishness', a way of laying bare the distortions that fuel anti-Semitism, replacing them with a more balanced account of what it is like to be a minority in an established society.

Jews (in spite of a long-held belief that they are the 'chosen people') will normally make no claim to be more than a cross-section of the society where they live. They come in all shapes and sizes. But all share a common background – inheriting a long history of uncertainty, moving from one country to another, often fleeing persecution. With such a troubled history, the closeness of family and community has remained at the heart of Jewish life. And always there is the irresistible dream of freedom.

My family was fortunate in finding its way to England, often by chance and along separate pathways, from different parts of the world. And it is here that we have found the very freedom to be ourselves that had for so long been sought. It was a good move (or, more accurately, series of moves). This country has proved a generous host and we are overwhelmingly loyal and thankful in return. I hope, above all, that this message of commitment comes across loud and clear.

Acknowledgements

People lead busy lives and it is never easy to find enough time to search the records for one's family history. There is no ideal moment to embark on such a venture; as one of the contributors to this project wryly observed, 'now that I'm retired, I don't have much time to spend on this sort of thing'. I know the feeling!

But, fortunately, curiosity has prevailed and precious time has been found by various individuals to set out on a journey of discovery; and it has been a great privilege to be entrusted with the task of piecing together some of the many fragments that they have contributed.

My cousin, Lesley Abdela, with her distinctive surname and high-profile presence as a champion of women's rights, has long attracted enquiries about her family background and has been an important source of inspiration and knowledge. Lesley, in turn, has inspired her son, Nick Hole, to take up the baton and his contribution is warmly acknowledged.

Tim Moss has collected some helpful documents about his own side of the extended family, and these have been gratefully received. Sincere thanks to Tim. So, too, my cousins, Lawrence Beilin and David Sagar, for valuable information and fascinating anecdotes. Barbara Wicks, tells of the eventful life of a branch of the Abdelas in southern Africa; while Justin Shasha has filled in some of the details of his own family's journey from Baghdad. I am grateful, as well, to my elder son, Rowan, and daughter, Gemma, for describing their stories of working on a kibbutz when they were students.

It will be seen from the above that I owe a great debt to all of those relatives who have helped me along the way. I usually refer in the text to 'my', rather than 'our', family, simply because it would not always be clear who is included in the latter. Certainly, no sleight is intended to other family members. Poetic license, if you will, that I hope will be understood.

Most of all, I would like to thank my wife, Jane, who wondered why I had not previously made my own enquiries and was determined to put this right. As a result, she has spent countless hours chasing down every last detail about the families in question, refusing to give up when the clues ran out. She would have made an outstanding detective. Jane has also handled the many photos and other illustrations that are included in the book. Only I am aware of the time and care she has devoted to this project and the constant support she has given me. By rights, she should be credited as co-author but her preference is to be acknowledged as principal researcher and designer – and so it is.

Finally, I can only wish that everyone mentioned in the intricately connected families, the source of inspiration for this book, could be with us and know that they have not been forgotten. This is their story and I am sure that all of the present generations would agree that this record be devoted to their enduring memory. And to Jews everywhere.

Glossary

aliyah	the Zionist call to return to the land of Israel
Ashkenazim	Jews who lived originally in the German states and neighbouring areas of Europe and developed their own practices
bar mitzvah	Jewish initiation ceremony for a boy
bat mitzvah	Jewish initiation ceremony for a girl
diaspora	the geographical spread of Jews beyond their original homeland
emancipation	used in the sense of liberation from restrictions imposed on Jews in host countries
Eretz Yisrael	refers to what Jews regard as their homeland
kippah	a skullcap worn as a head-covering in honour to God
mikveh	designated bath for Jews to attain ritual purification
minyan	quorum of ten (traditionally men) required to enable Jewish public worship
mitzvah	commandment
Mizrahim	descendants of Jewish communities in the Middle East and North Africa, living there from biblical times through to the modern era
Pale of Settlement	region of western Russia where Jews were allowed to settle: but not beyond the Pale

phylactery	small leather box containing scrolls of parchment with verses from the Torah, carried by men and used in morning prayer
pogrom	attack on Jewish lives and properties in eastern Europe and Russia
Romaniotes	the oldest Jewish community of the diaspora, dating back to settlements in Greece even before the Christian era
Sephardi(m)	Jewish ethnic group originating from Spain and Portugal
shtetl	small Jewish town or village in eastern Europe (mainly Russia)
shul	synagogue (Yiddish)
shtiebel	a small place used for communal Jewish prayer, often before a synagogue was built
Talmud	the major text of the Jewish tradition, the scholarly work of rabbis
Torah	the teaching or law handed down to Moses on Mount Sinai
tsedakah	Hebrew word for charity and philanthropy
yarmulke	as for kippah
Yiddish	hybrid language, mainly a mix of German and Hebrew

Introduction

My Family and Other Jews[1]

If this were just another family history, I would expect most readers to stop here. Such monographs are invariably only of interest to the subjects in question. Aunt Genevieve's praiseworthy trek up the slopes of Mount Kilimanjaro at the age of 90, and young Toby's Olympian achievements on the running track, cut little ice with those of us outside the magic circle. Family trees are, in any case, enormously complex and too often require the skills of a cryptologist to decode them. Readers, please be assured that this modest volume is *not* in that traditional mould.

Instead, what is intended is to give a sense of being Jewish in England over the past few centuries and, not least of all, in the present day. This has been a momentous period for everyone, Jews and non-Jews alike, but for the former there has always been an added dimension. It was only in the middle of the seventeenth century that Jews were allowed once again to settle in this country. They had lived in England before but (after little more than 200 years) were expelled in 1290. There was no choice but to seek other places where they hoped to be accepted. Wherever it was, however, life was never easy and persecution followed them from country to country like a hunting dog.

The freedom to settle and practice their beliefs without let or hindrance was an alluring prospect. Was there such a place on the map? Returning to England when the opportunity arose suggested there might be. To this country's great credit, there is no record over the past few centuries of the massacres that periodically devastated Jewish communities in central and eastern Europe, and in neighbouring Russia. The level of hatred for Jews in that part of the world was unremitting and only reached a climax in the twentieth century, in the unprecedented events of the Nazi Holocaust.

In contrast, England was one of the few countries in modern Europe which could offer respite. If Jewish immigrants could afford to do so, they were free to build synagogues and to practice their religion as they wished. And unlike in the first phase of Jewish settlement (when they could only be moneylenders), they could now pursue any number of occupations of their choosing. They could buy land and, in the great industrial centres, there were numerous business opportunities. They could cook their own food, obey the disciplines of their sabbath and celebrate religious festivals in peace. From time to time, they might well hear the occasional negative comment and aside, but, in the main, they lived without fear.

Given this degree of tolerance, it is not surprising that many Jews found their way to 'this blessed plot', my own ancestors amongst them. Countries elsewhere in the British Isles attracted Jewish migrants too but it so happened that the characters in this particular story chose to settle in England; mainly in London and Manchester, cities known across the world for their industry and commerce.

So what was it like to be a Jew in England, when they first arrived, and what is it like now? Has the experience changed over the years? Is Jewishness an enduring feature or has a long process of assimilation blurred the edges? If it worked well in the past, why is there presently new evidence of anti-Semitism? Why do so many Jews currently feel uneasy when they have enjoyed security for so long? Is this the same country that, alone amongst European neighbours, kept the threat of extermination at bay? What has changed?

In order to explore these general questions, it is necessary to go beyond the narrow boundaries of a traditional ancestral search. That is why I have placed the experience of settling in England in the context of a broader understanding of how Jews came to be as they are. Successive chapters deal with different themes, starting with the original diaspora and touching on issues of recurring interest, like the strength of community and the place of business. I have turned to members of my own extended family, past and present, for examples of how they addressed these issues. The history of individual families provides insights into everything that follows. This relationship between the stories of my own relatives and wider currents of change is at the very heart of the book. The outcome is family history turned upside down, as an illustrator of events rather than an end in itself.

Delving into the past is no easy task for any researcher and, not least of all, if the subject is Jewish history, where evidence is both patchy and dispersed. Over the two millennia of the diaspora, records have been lost and, in many cases, wilfully destroyed. There were legendary scribes like the scholarly Rabbi Benjamin of Tudela who, in the twelfth century, embarked on a journey that took him eastwards from Spain across Europe to western Asia, not to mention forays into North Africa, visiting Jewish communities along the way. It was a monumental achievement to do what he did, yet even he could offer only a very partial picture. For anything more comprehensive, synagogue records would need to be consulted but, from one century to another, the synagogues themselves have largely disappeared.

The paucity of records is an irretrievable loss and has necessarily limited the scope of this project. Or, indeed, any other attempt to recall Jewish family history. There is little I have been able to find about my own ancestors which takes me back beyond the eighteenth century. Two or three hundred years of history might not seem much in the scheme of things, but even that has been challenging enough – a time of enormous change in the world, with intriguing stories of individual families.

To add to the challenge, I have had to learn something about the popular subject of genealogy. I think the first lesson was to discover that the process of finding out about one's ancestors is a quicksand for the unwary. The ground looks firm and there must surely be well-trodden tracks to follow, but nothing is as it seems. Identical names lure many an explorer in a wrong direction. Cross-checking and forensic attention to detail is the only way to stand a chance of staying on course. Yet even then one is relying on records which may themselves be wrong; we can never be certain that those who provided the information in the first place did so correctly and conscientiously. We can never be sure that firsthand accounts are not embroidered with exaggeration or flawed by the omission of uncomfortable facts. As a result, family history is not an exact science but, with patience, one can at least emerge with useful pictures of who was who, and how things were. And no-one can deny that it is an absorbing pursuit, a quest to find links with a distant past that one can help to piece together.

Difficult though it is, at least now there are valuable sources of information that can be reached from the comfort of one's own home. Making time-consuming journeys to different parts of the country, and to other countries as well, only to find that what you were looking for is missing, is largely a thing of the past. In any case, even if the information is there, links can sometimes be remarkably elusive, made more difficult by the similarity of so many names in a family.

In the story that follows we have to disentangle the likes of Moses Joseph and Joseph Moses, and be sure we know the difference between the grandma who is a Goodman and a dear aunt with the married name of Badmann; as a young boy I was never quite sure who was a Rosie and who a Rosetta; we have to distinguish Shasha and Shashoua; and to know which surnames were changed in the course of a lifetime (invariably to sound less Jewish but also to escape anti-German sentiment in the two world wars). By rights, my own surname should be Simon but my paternal grandfather, Hardy Simon, reversed the order of his names. And my middle name, Isaac, was rarely revealed.

In writing the narrative, to avoid unnecessary confusion I have tried to limit the number of family names, introducing them only to illustrate general themes. Suffice to say at this point (as we can see in the box that follows) that the principal characters to begin the search comprise immediate members of four families: Abdela, Moss, Hardy and Goodman.

Abdela/Moss/Hardy/Goodman

What's in a Name?

I start the story with my grandparents:

> On my mother's side, *Isaac Abdela* married *Sophia Moss*; and for the paternal link, *Hardy Simon* (later *Simon Hardy*) married *Julia Goodman*.

I have used these as markers for what would otherwise be an unstructured journey. It is rather like the four points of a compass which can send the traveller in different directions, without necessarily having to know every place in between. No matter how far back in time a connection is found, nor whether the link is direct through blood lineage or indirect through marriage, all of my relatives can identify with one of these four family names. From this starting point, I make journeys backwards and forwards, as well as across to related families. There is no need to know more about these leading actors at this stage nor about the supporting cast. The storyline that follows does not make this essential. However, for those who might want to pursue this, I have included a short supplement to the main text, under the heading of 'Compass Points'. This is intended to provide a little more information about the connections between these principal families and to links beyond.

With the above in mind, there is a single question that has intrigued me for much of my life. Quite simply, what was it that, independently, brought my ancestors from various parts of the world to make their home in an island nation off the coast of continental Europe? Was it luck or judgement that spared them from annihilation during the Second World War? Not many Jewish families emerged intact in 1945; most would have stories of close relatives who failed to survive. Yet (apart from those who died fighting for their adopted country) mine were all there at the end of the conflict, fit and ready to engage in a postwar revolution of economic and social change, a new chapter in Jewish history. I would like to know what decisions were taken at different times in the past that led them to this point. Sadly, for all my curiosity, I wish that I had probed this question more deeply with relatives while I could have done so.

Although, in the true spirit of such exploration, I have done my very best to make the account as accurate as possible, I have readily acknowledged where there are gaps in the evidence. This, of course, is an occupational hazard that historians regularly bemoan. The records in certain cases no longer exist and there is little one can do, other than to speculate on the basis of general trends. Some of the evidence I have turned to is, inevitably, circumstantial. For this, I am indebted to the authors of the many books on Jewish history that provide a reliable context (and which I acknowledge in the subsequent text).

Foibles apart, as an ulterior motive in writing this book I can only hope that the text will reveal, in some small way, the sheer folly of anti-Semitism. Why are Jews, time and again, singled out for special treatment? Why is there presently a resurgence of vindictiveness? We represent a very small minority of the world population, yet are treated disproportionately as a subject of abuse. Race, religion, geopolitics and identity are used by anti-Semites to make their point. In the rest of this book, opportunities abound for readers to assess the basis for the various accusations. I can hardly pretend to be dispassionate about the issues but I have tried, as far as possible, to let others decide what is right and what is wrong. This book is not about me but about my extended family and, more widely, about Jews in England. It is their stories that count.

So, it is time now to consider the evidence, to immerse oneself in Jewish history and then let family members tell us what it meant to them. As a result, I hope we will get at least a glimpse of what it has meant (and still does) to be a Jew in England.

Chapter 1

Diaspora

The gardeners amongst you may be familiar with an ubiquitous plant, known by its scientific name as *Tradescantia* but more commonly through one of its species, Wandering Jew. Originating in Mexico and Central America, it is quite resilient to different conditions, growing well indoors as a house plant or outdoors in domestic gardens. Its violet blooms are small, with three petals, and leaves are variegated (hence the full name of the species, *Tradescantia Zebrina*). The plant itself grows easily and it is not hard to see why it is referred to as 'wandering'. But where does the Jewish descriptor come in?

The story has it that Jews were held responsible, not just for complicity in the crucifixion of Christ, but for taunting him on his way to the cross. For this, many Christians were unforgiving, in turn creating a legend that Jews should be cast out and forced to suffer until the end of time. By the time that Christianity was firmly established and documented, it could then be seen as sinful to reject this unquestionable truth. For these different reasons, from one century to the next, hatred of the Jews remained a potent force. In the seventeenth and eighteenth centuries, for instance, there were numerous texts, most originating in the German states, confirming this conflict of beliefs and stoking the fires of resentment. Unintentionally, however, the accusers raised the possibility that their perennial condemnation might also be interpreted as a sign of the enduring strength of those they sought to punish. Thus, in a reference to the legend in the *Jewish Encyclopaedia* of 1906, Joseph Jacobs wrote:

> *The figure of the doomed sinner, forced to wander without the hope of rest in death till the millennium, impressed itself upon the popular imagination, and passed thence into literary art, mainly with reference to the seeming immortality of the wandering Jewish race.*[2]

For two thousand years, Jews have been on the move. But, against all odds, they have refused to succumb; instead, in the above words, they have demonstrated 'the seeming immortality of the wandering Jewish race'.

If this general thesis seems a little abstract, one only has to look more closely at the different stories of the families that feature in this book. Time and again there is a record of journeys, of moving from one country to another and even crossing continents. If we start with my own grandparents, each comes from a different place: my paternal grandfather from Germany and his wife from an immigrant community in east London (and before that, also from continental Europe), my maternal grandmother from Canada and her husband from Corfu. As we delve deeper into the origins of earlier ancestors and extended family members who came to England, it reads like a gazetteer, with lines on the map tracing journeys from Poland and Austria, Syria and Iraq, Holland and Alsace, Egypt and Ukraine, and from Ottoman Turkey and Russia. Nor was it all one way, with subsequent moves from Europe to Australia (not always by choice, as the records of convict transportation show) and the United States, southern Africa and South America. But, markedly, not to Israel, a fact that cannot be allowed to rest without later questions.

As the following anecdote illustrates, the complexity of origins is invariably taken for granted and is largely invisible in everyday relations.

Moss

Convoluted Journeys

Aunt Rosalind (known as Rosie) and Uncle Meyer lived in a grand apartment with high ceilings, facing the seafront in Brighton. The one was my maternal grandmother's sister and the other her second husband. On Sunday afternoon visits, the door would be opened by a maid in uniform, who would show us to the living room before preparing a tray of tea and cake. I would be seated in a chair by a floor-to-ceiling window so that I could look at the sea while the adults gossiped.

Rosie was born in 1882, shortly after her family had moved to England from Canada. She first married a Syrian merchant from Aleppo, but he died in 1912 on a business trip to Alexandria. After a few years, Rosie married again, this time to Meyer Samuel Dubowski.

I never knew where the couple had met but learned later that Meyer grew up in humble circumstances in the East End, although he had since made good in the world of business. His main venture was as a wholesale dairy supplier but he also owned grocery shops in that part of London.

The records show that his family came originally from western Russia, part of a wider region where boundaries have slipped at different times between Poland, Belarus and Lithuania. Whatever his origins, I recall him as an imposing figure with a brush moustache, wearing a suit to match the formality of the occasion. I liked him, not least of all because when we left to return to London at the end of the afternoon, he would always press a half crown into the palm of my hand. Young boys never forget things like that.

Visits to Rosie and Meyer were made after the passing in 1945 of my grandmother, Birdie Abdela. I would have been five or six at the time, too young to have a sense of the convoluted origins of the people we were visiting. Canada, Syria, Russia and England were interwoven threads that told their own story of the Jewish diaspora. Little wonder that I would later spend hours collecting stamps of exotic places and, at school and university, studying Geography.

From one generation to the next, individual decisions were made to relocate but, more often than not, these were framed in the context of general trends in the diaspora. So why did our ancestors go where they did and to what extent were these journeys really part of broader movements? How was it that they eventually made their way to England?

The Jewish odyssey begins in biblical times, in the semi-arid strip of land that follows the Mediterranean coast between present-day Egypt and Lebanon, very broadly corresponding with modern Israel. It is this that Jews have always regarded as their homeland, even though for most of the later generations it remained a place of imagination.

A Question of Identity

Wherever a Jew lived, in whatever safety and isolation, he still belonged to his people.[3]

Diaspora is a generic term used to describe any process of population dispersal which takes people away from an original homeland. In modern terms, reference to the Chinese or Indian diaspora is commonplace and everyone knows what it means. Equally, the Jewish diaspora has a universal meaning and the process is very much at the heart of this book. Families were swept along in its wake, like pebbles carried up and down the beach by the tide, with little choice where they came to rest – nor whether the next high tide would move them on again.

If, at first, the definition of diaspora sounds relatively straightforward, the meaning in the case of the Jewish dispersal is, in fact, enormously complex. No-one who is Jewish can fail to empathize with what their ancestors must have endured, moving from place to place, asking for no more than the freedom to lead their various lives in peace. But theirs has been a ceaseless journey, where hopes were repeatedly dashed. Each time they thought they had found permanent relief, circumstances changed and it was time once again to pack their meagre belongings. No matter how weary, there was no option but to continue their search elsewhere. They showed remarkable fortitude. At the very least, one owes our ancestors the debt of telling their unique story, of trying to recreate the various journeys that led them, eventually, to where we are now.

But where should we start? 'Start at the beginning and go on until the end – and then stop' was the cryptic advice given to Alice on her journey in Wonderland. Yet where was the beginning and how does one know when one reaches the end? And is there an end? More likely, the start of a new, as yet unwritten, chapter.

Retracing how it all began takes us back a very long way, into the lost and largely illusory world of Moses and the Ten Commandments, perhaps as much as 3500 years ago. That is also where one finds the 600 or so instructions on how to conduct one's life, brought together by the first rabbis in the Torah and recorded in the opening five books of the Old Testament, the Jewish bible. In this distant world of pre-history, one finds interwoven stories of nomadic tribes scratching out a living in the desert fringes of the eastern Mediterranean, mainly the two adjoining provinces of Judaea and Israel. There were periods of servitude and, even then, exile, but the central tenet of their belief – that there was only one God – was firmly established from this early era.

Known as the Israelites (or, more commonly in later history, the Jews), their nomadic life gradually evolved into a more settled existence, with the emergence of kings to provide leadership. King David brought inspiration and Solomon (in the middle of the tenth century BCE) is renowned not only for his wisdom but also for the building of the iconic Temple in Jerusalem, where all the teachings were stored in the Ark of the Covenant. Even at the time, there were those who wondered if Solomon had exceeded himself, putting grandeur ahead of religious purpose. The Ark of the Covenant was no more than a wooden chest containing the tablets of the Torah, yet in the new temple it was almost lost amidst gold chains descending from the roof, soaring columns of brass, with walls and floors faced with scented cedar from Lebanon, and intricate wood carvings embellished with more gold. To true believers it resembled a pagan place of worship rather than the home of a religion owing its very being to an omnipotent God; to a modern reader it might just as easily describe a seven-star hotel in Dubai. Is this what religion is all about?

For all the doubts, however, completion of the Temple marked the end of an unprecedented process of construction and also the beginning of a new era of religious identity, for 'the Temple was not just a shrine, it was the home of God himself'.[4] It might have seemed then that territory and beliefs had come together, twin pillars of a combination of race and religion, the birth of a nation. But that was not to be, and midway through the first millennium BCE, any thoughts of a stable nation state were violently erased by the invading Babylonians. Their superior armies, advancing from the fertile river valleys of the Tigris and Euphrates to the east, were more than a match for the Jews. The invaders destroyed the Temple and took many of the indigenous Jews to work as slaves in their own country. This was a pivotal moment in Jewish history, perhaps even the very point which marks the start of the diaspora. In the words of one expert on the subject:

> *The exiles maintained their attachment to the old country, and their hope of an eventual return. They also clung to their national identity, and from this time on Judaism effectively lost its territorial basis... The communities preserved their distinct identity based on a common past and strengthened through family and clan loyalties. The idea of the nation was no longer linked directly to territory: God's rule extended to the whole world, even if Jerusalem was his special home.[5]*

In fact, it was not such a decisive moment as it first appears, as the seemingly invincible Babylonians fell, in due course, to a Persian conquest and, much to the surprise of the Jews, the new ruler, King Darius, ordered the rebuilding of the hallowed Temple. It was a calculated move, designed to buy peace within his empire, and his successors honoured his wish. The outcome, however, the Second Temple, was a pale reflection of the original edifice and the Jewish community had to wait another five centuries before their hopes for what was seen as a more fitting place of worship could be met. Any lingering fears that the simplicity of their beliefs would be overwhelmed by another exhibition of material splendour were then largely unvoiced.

This time it was the Jewish king, Herod, who met the challenge. He removed what was left of the Second Temple in order to put in its place a structure that would leave no doubt about his intentions:

> *A thousand priests were trained as builders. Lebanese cedar forests were felled, the beams floated down the coast. At quarries around Jerusalem, the massive ashlar stones, gleaming yellow and almost white limestone, were marked and cut out. A thousand wagons were amassed but the stones were gargantuan.*[6]

No expense was spared to build a Temple that would last a thousand years. But Herod ignored the fact that Jerusalem had already shown itself to be vulnerable to foreign powers. In his own lifetime, he would have known that the security of the Temple was dependent on the dictates of the Romans, who came to control the whole region as part of their own powerful empire. It was probably not a wise move to challenge Roman authority and an unsuccessful revolt soon provoked a reversal of quiet Jewish progress, including the destruction once again of their beloved Temple.

By the time of that event, in 70 CE, the belief that there were surely less troubled places to settle had taken root. The figures tell their own story. In spite of its chequered start, in terms of numbers, Judaism, by the time of Christ, had become a force to be reckoned with:

> *Shortly before 70 CE there were over two and a half million Jews in Judaea and well over four million in the Roman diaspora. Subsequently... the ratio of diaspora to Palestinian Jewry increased considerably. It is likely that the Jews represented something like a tenth of the whole population of the empire.*[7]

There was still a chance that they would be tolerated as a state within a state but, with the later conversion of the Romans to Christianity, an acceptance of Jews in the Roman Empire became less likely. Quite apart from their betrayal of Christ, it became inconceivable that they would be allowed to openly spurn the sanctity of Christian beliefs. Although Roman control was to end in the fifth century, many Jews had by then already left their original homeland. The diaspora was well underway, with families first moving to cities within what was later known as the Near and Middle East, and then in a different direction, to the states of western and southern Europe. This latter movement ushered in a process that was to become all too familiar, of Jews making their homes in places like France and Spain, England and Portugal, only to be expelled and forced to move on again. For the best part of two millennia, the constant movement that marked the diaspora was to be an essential part of Jewish history.

The exiled Jews took their religion with them, and also a yearning to return one day to what they regarded as their homeland. Surely, they maintained, a return was ordained, for had not the Lord himself promised Abraham that:

> *I will give unto thee, and to thy seed after thee, the land wherein thou art a stranger, all the land of Canaan.*[8]

This was enough to give rise to the enduring concept of the Promised Land, the hidden magnet which, wherever they settled, constantly drew the thoughts of Jews back to the place of their origins. No matter that the boundaries of the land in question were vague in the extreme, the very prospect of a place to return to – underwritten by God – was enough to nourish the wandering people in their darkest hours.

Hardy

Next Year in Jerusalem

In some ways, in writing this book on behalf of my extended family I feel something of an impostor. The religious side of being Jewish has never taken a hold on me and even the lure of the homeland gives rise to mixed thoughts. But if anyone asks if I *feel* Jewish, the answer is unquestionably so. Why would one ask?

Perhaps, if this seems contradictory, I have to explain that I grew up in a Jewish household where the main religious festivals were observed. As a young boy, their meaning probably came second to their enjoyment. And none was more enjoyable than the annual Passover service, the Seder. While my father read his lines from the Haggadah in Hebrew, I would turn the pages in my own, illustrated book to see when we would next break off to taste one of the delicious dishes for the occasion prepared by my mother. These were all symbolic, like apple sauce and cinnamon to represent the mortar used by the Jews in Egypt, and the bitterness of horseradish as a reminder of the hardship of slavery, an egg to welcome spring, and, of course, unleavened bread (matzoh) for when there was no time to complete the baking of bread when escaping captivity. Not to mention my sanctified introduction to glasses of red wine!

I would look at the pictures in my book – of Moses in the bull-rushes by the Nile, of the parting of the Red Sea, and of kibbutznik planting trees in the modern Jewish state. The image of turning a desert into farmland made a deep impression. My flights of fancy were only interrupted by times when we all recited one line or another in the service, the one I remember best being at the end of the Seder, 'Next year in Jerusalem'. Everyone was contemplative, each with their own thoughts, myself included.

The sense of being Jewish is not easily defined. It goes beyond adherence to a set of essential beliefs: a belief in one God which, when the idea was first broached, was in sharp contrast to obeisance to multiple idols; a recognition that Judaism can be both a religion and a race, or for many people even just one or the other; an acceptance that one day in the week must be observed as the sabbath; and an unwritten desire to return to the homeland, based loosely on the historic provinces of Judaea and Israel, and always including the holy city of Jerusalem. In their endless journeys across continents, not all of these beliefs would have been uppermost in their minds. But the feeling of being Jewish never went away; without that belief it is unlikely that they would have survived.

As I know from my own experience, Jews are naturally argumentative and even a seemingly uncontentious definition like the above would not be allowed to pass without animated questioning. How can I be a Jew in the synagogue but then shun a commitment to my homeland – surely it has to be religion *and* race? Can there be anything other than an orthodox reading of the Torah if one is to sustain Jewish integrity? Given the endless history of persecution, is there really any other option but to live together in Israel?

But why argue? The very process of taking issue over one point or another misses the fact that no-one is questioning whether they are Jewish. The questions are all about defining a position within the same realm of thought. More fruitful, I believe, is to take the view that identity is what you feel it is. My ancestors have made me what I am and I owe them a debt. Likewise, it is important that my children, and theirs too, know that they come from the same lineage, even if this is now more tenuous because of repeated intermarriage.

Perhaps the most powerful reminder of our identity comes, not from what we have read or been told, but from a constant threat of persecution. It is ironic that this, throughout the diaspora, has been a unifying force, contrary to the aims of successive persecutors. Rather than dissembling in the face of repeated attacks from one source or another – physical, verbal and by ordinance – the Jewish faith was strengthened. Jews have refused to give way, and their consciousness of being who they are has grown more resilient.

That is why the ties of family and community remain so important, staying close to others who share essential qualities and beliefs, when they are confronted by hostile outsiders. Even in times of relative tranquility, old ways die hard and Jews feel more comfortable if they are not far away from others of their kind. It is almost a sense of pride, telling the rest of the world that 'we're here, we've made it'.

Hardy

Jewish Pride

At one time, a distant relative, Mossy Lazarus, lodged with my family. His wife, Lydia, had died some years before and Mossy cut a lonely figure, though his demeanour visibly brightened on a Saturday when he walked from our house to watch his beloved Hendon Football Club. Always conscious of his own Jewishness (but seeing no contradiction in going to a football match on the sabbath) it gave him special pride to tell me that one of the players, Miles Spector, was 'one of us'.

Spector was a strong player, usually on the wing, and a prolific goal-scorer. His main claim to fame was to appear in a number of games for Chelsea. He excelled at all levels but for most of his playing career he stayed as an amateur with Hendon. Mossy would return from the latest match with news of Spector's performance. To round off his report, I could be sure that he would conclude with the words, 'he's a Yiddisher boy, you know'.

Not so many 'Yiddisher boys' have made a career for themselves in football, although David Beckham reminds us that he had a Jewish grandfather.

Mossy clearly felt his Jewishness keenly. As far as I know, he was not religious in a conventional sense, and, clearly, the weekly sabbath was not a time for quiet reflection and prayer. But his sense of identity was sharply honed, although never defined in specific terms. In contrast, the issue of identity is one that presently occupies many pages in academic journals, columns of newspapers, and air time on talk shows. It has taken its place most recently alongside other identity issues, like race, gender and sexuality.

But, as the above anecdote illustrates, it is nothing new and has for centuries been at the heart of the Jewish question, for both good and ill. Jews define themselves and their families by who they are, and, from the outside, others do the same. No matter that they might be contributing to society, whether in peacetime or war, there will always be those who continue to dismiss Jews as an alien race. Jewish identity has constantly had to confront opposing views at one and the same time.

Journeys

It is a curious fact that for more than three-quarters of their existence as a race,
a majority of Jews have always lived outside the land they call their own.[9]

On leaving their homeland, Jews set out in different directions. Along
the way they became familiar with new cultures, adopting some features
and discarding others. Their food and clothing reflected where they
found themselves as well as what they had brought with them. They
learned new languages but never forgot the old. And even their religious
practices saw changes, most importantly in the two main groupings of
Sephardi and Ashkenazi, but also in the practices of smaller factions. As
we will see, different journeys brought different outcomes; the diaspora
was a kaleidoscope of contrasts, though always with a common core of
emotions, the feeling of being Jewish. It was perhaps unavoidable that
the long trek across continents gave rise to important differences in
tradition and practice. Yet, through it all, the remarkable fact is that
neither religion nor race diminished in intensity.

Finding Sanctuary in Greece

For some Jews, the writing was already on the wall as early as the destruction
of the First Temple by the Babylonians. Over a long period, and hastened
by the destruction of the Second Temple in 70 CE, a succession of Jews
made the decision to leave their homeland and to seek somewhere safer to
live. For some of these pioneering exiles, one of the earliest destinations
was along the northern coastline of the Mediterranean.

They followed the seaboard of what later became the modern nation of
Greece, initially making homes in the cities of Corinth and Patra. Later,
they wended their way in a north-westerly direction, through towns and
villages facing the Ionian Sea. A number of families (including some of
my own ancestors) were attracted in this way to the small, coastal town
of Arta.

When the Jewish scholar, Benjamin of Tudela, made his epic journey from
Spain to Jerusalem in the twelfth century, it is recorded that:

> *… after leaving Corfu he went to Arta, where he found a Jewish*
> *community of 100 families who led a rich spiritual and religious life.*

He also noted that this was during the reign of the Byzantine Emperor, Manuel Kominos II, and that the leaders of the Jewish community of Arta were Rabbi Solomon and Rabbi Heracles.[10]

It was, in fact, during the Byzantine period that the first synagogue in Arta was built. The original settlers were joined in the thirteenth century by Jews from Corfu, who fled the nearby island to avoid being caught up in a conflict between Robert of Sicily and the Byzantines.

In their new communities, they fashioned a distinctive branch of Judaism and were later known as the Romaniotes. They spoke Greek (albeit a form of Greek infused with Hebrew) and developed their own religious practices. For centuries their presence was tolerated in the region, first by the Christian Byzantines and then the Ottoman Turks. The latter, especially, appreciated the contribution that the Jews could make to commerce and a successful economy, where they played a leading role as merchants and ship-owners.

With the expulsion of the Spanish Jews from their adopted country in 1492, it might have been thought that the community in Arta would have been joined by migrants from Iberia but, instead, it was mainly from Italy that new arrivals came. One reason, it is believed, is that Italian Jews found it easier to adapt to the Romaniote liturgy, which had acquired its own idiosyncrasies. Yet, if there was a certain synergy between the two it did not prevent the Italians building their own place of worship in Arta, called the Pugliese Synagogue.[11]

Abdela

Ionian Refuge

It is not known for how long they lived in Arta, but one of the Jewish families highlighted in this book, the Abdelas, was certainly in residence in the 1830s. There is also an interesting reference to the fact that much earlier, in 1622, a Samuel Abdela had successfully acted as envoy to the Doge in Venice (to which this area owed allegiance). Representing the Jewish community, he made pleas against the imminent threat of repressive sanctions.[12] Lydia Collins, the acknowledged expert of Sephardi families from this region who later came to live in England, believes that the Abdelas were 'probably of Romaniote origin'.[13] Given the long history of Jewish settlement along that coastline, there is no obvious reason to doubt this.

 When he was still a boy, young Jacob Elia Abdela (born in Arta in 1838 or 1839) moved with his family to Corfu. They were one of a number of other Jewish families who made the same move. The reason for the exodus across the narrow neck of the Ionian Sea was almost certainly connected with the fact that, following the Napoleonic Wars, Corfu was ceded to Britain. In the minds of Jews in the region at the time, being part of the British Empire offered a more stable environment than continuing to live in what had, by then, become the disputed territory of Arta. The Greek War of Independence, in which Hellenic nationalists fought the Ottoman rulers, ended in 1829 in favour of the new nation state of Greece. But boundaries with the now-diminished Turkish Empire were far from settled, so much so that Arta itself remained for another half century within the Ottoman regime. In fact, it was not until 1881 that it was finally ceded to Greece. Given so many uncertainties, one can see why Jacob Elia's parents made the decision to move from Arta to Corfu.

By all accounts, Corfu was a good move for the Abdelas, and Jacob Elia grew up to be a successful businessman and an established member of the Jewish community. There was no more meaningful sign of success in Jewish circles than becoming president of one's synagogue, which was the honour bestowed on him. Before he was thirty, he married a Jewish woman from Corfu, Miriam Mostachi, and the couple parented a family of seven children (six sons and one daughter). Only three of these – Suvi, Elia and Isaac – were born in Corfu. Following a move to England in the mid-1870s, the birthplace of the younger children – Rachel, Raphael, Joseph and Robert – was to be Manchester.

Most Romaniotes, however, remained in Greece, not only in Arta but in other parts of the new nation state too; Ioannina, for instance, a mountain settlement in north-western Greece, was an important centre for Romaniote culture. At one time, more than 4000 Jews lived in Ioannina, although by the eve of the Second World War this number had dwindled to nearer 2000. An important reason for the smaller number was a common decision to emigrate, especially to the United States, to escape perennial poverty. Those who did so were to prove fortunate in another way too when, in 1944, centuries of living in peace in the Greek mountain community were to end in the worst possible way:

> *On March 25, 1944, the German Nazi occupiers rounded up the Jews of Ioannina. As snow fell, they were put into open trucks and taken to a nearby city. From there, a nine-day rail journey took them to Auschwitz. The names of the town's 1,832 Jews who were murdered are carved on marble tablets on the walls of the synagogue. Among the dead were more than 500 children under the age of 13. Only 112 Ioannina Jews survived the death camps.*[14]

The tiny community that was left has never recovered. People visit the site today for what it was, not for what it is, recalling just one of many dreadful acts of persecution. Elsewhere in the world, Romaniotes have largely settled for a quiet existence alongside the Sephardim, attending the same synagogues and seeing themselves as an integral part of the latter.

Cabo Finisterra

Meanwhile, other Jews had left the homeland with a different destination in mind. Skirting the shores of Greece, large numbers of Jews sailed westwards on crowded ships in their own determined quest to find salvation. There were points along the way where they might have hoped to settle but, one after the other, they found they were not welcome. Sometimes they secured a temporary refuge but it was not long before they were ordered to leave, driven out by religious prejudice or local traders who feared they could not compete with the newcomers. Their last port of call was the Iberian Peninsula, where, finally, they were given the opportunity to settle and prosper.

This respite could not have come too soon and a map would show that there was nowhere further west to go. On the far north-western coast is

Cabo Finisterra, literally meaning the end of the world, facing the hostile and largely unknown Atlantic Ocean. It is a coincidence that in 1492, the same year that the Jews were eventually expelled from Spain, an Italian navigator, Christopher Columbus, would lead an expedition from a Spanish port to find what lay over the horizon. The New World would later draw Jews in their hundreds of thousands, providing a permanent escape from European animosity, but, when they first arrived in Spain, that possibility was far beyond reach. Their reliance on Spain to provide refuge was total.

For as long as it lasted, they were to do well in both Spain and neighbouring Portugal, finding an understanding with the dominant Moors and engaging in the arts as well as commerce. But as soon as the Moors were defeated and sent back across the sea to North Africa, the triumphant Catholics ordered the expulsion of the Jews as well. Rather than leave the country, many chose the option of converting to Christianity but others, unwilling to do this, found themselves on the move once again. Just a few years after the Spanish decree was passed, Portugal did the same; although here, if they wanted to stay, Jews were forced rather than given the option to convert. In both countries, even if they converted, they were still regarded with suspicion, to a point where leaving became a necessity.

So now the original direction of the diaspora was reversed and ships sailed, this time, back towards the east. Some of the exiles sought refuge in countries along the North African coastline, starting with Morocco, where the port of Tétouan attracted a large number of new-wave immigrants. At one stage, Tétouan had as many as sixteen synagogues but in the face of growing opposition to the Jewish presence, by 1948 all but a few families found it safe to remain. Egypt also attracted its own migrants, direct from the provinces of Judaea and Israel, lured by opportunities for trade at a natural junction of continents; the ancient city of Alexandria, in particular, was a popular point of arrival.

Meanwhile, along the northern Mediterranean coastline, the exiles from Iberia continued to look for places that would accept them. One popular refuge was the port of Livorno, on Italy's west coast, where a thriving Jewish community emerged. Further to the east, an accord was struck with the ruling Ottomans based in Constantinople. In spite of religious differences, the Muslim Turks found a synergy in working with the Jews and consolidating their own commercial interests in the eastern Mediterranean. A large Jewish community also gathered in Salonika and remained there until the Second World War, when, like the Romaniotes elsewhere in Greece, they were transported to camps in eastern Europe for mass slaughter.

Nearly 500 years elapsed between the time of their eviction from Iberia and the Second World War, and during that time numerous new communities were established. But many Jews had mixed feelings about remaining in the region and chose, instead, to join an earlier stream of exiles making their way overland to the east, in western Asia. In fact, some thought it timely to settle once again in the land they had originally left, the Promised Land, although even that proved not to be the welcoming place they had imagined. Others looked northwards to the cities of Aleppo and Damascus in Syria, and eastwards to Baghdad in Mesopotamia to start new lives; Baghdad, especially, offered many opportunities. Even more intrepid, some Jews ventured further east, to India, where they could play a part in the lucrative spice trade; visitors to the southern port of Cochin, for instance, can still see remnants in the old town of what was once a busy Jewish community.

Abdela/Moss

Eastern Promise

During the long – and almost certainly intermittent – journey to Spain and Portugal, and then the reverse voyage, there is no evidence that many of my ancestors were part of the main flows of migration. As Romaniotes, the Abdelas would have gone straight to Greece and settled there, missing out on the Iberian venture. Likewise, it is not apparent that there were early links with the Levant and Mesopotamia, although the name 'Abdela' does suggest an eastern provenance (Abdullah, or variations on this, being quite common amongst Iraqi Jews).

But all of that is speculative. What is not in doubt is that more recent family members created their own connections with the East through marriage. Rosalind Moss was a sister of my maternal grandmother and (as mentioned earlier in this chapter) her first marriage was to a man from Aleppo, Setton Nessim Menache.

Meanwhile, my maternal grandfather's sister, Rachel, was the only daughter in a family of seven children. In 1909 she married Joseph Shasha, who was born in Baghdad but had since come to live in Manchester. With a young relative of his, he went on to build a business as shippers to the Persian Gulf and Baghdad. Joseph and Rachel lived in south Manchester and were parents of five children. They left Manchester in 1938, on the eve of the Second World War, to live in Buenos Aires, only returning in 1948.

Of their five children, one of them was Jack Shasha who, in turn, married Pamela Garlick. Unusually in a time of strict protocols, this was a marriage out of the Jewish religion but he could not have chosen a better wife. Pam (as she was always known) was a spritely woman, with a great sense of fun. Her energy knew no bounds and, well into her 90s, she was still looking after her beloved Shetland ponies on her hillside land in the north-west of England. In the family records is a letter from Queen Elizabeth II, celebrating Pam's 100th birthday. The name of Shasha was carried forward through her son, Jonathan, and his own offspring, Justin and Caroline.

Another connection with the East came when my mother's sister, Iris, married Abraham Shashoua in Manchester in 1923. Abraham's family came originally from Baghdad, prior to moving to Manchester, where they established a company specializing in shipping cotton back to their home city.

In this whole episode of the diaspora – with voyages criss-crossing the Mediterranean, and an exploration of opportunities closer to the homeland – the expulsion of Jews from the Iberian Peninsula was a seminal event. Given that the Hebrew name for Spain was *Sepharad*, the whole group of migrants (whether from Spain or Portugal) were known as Sephardim. This came to have added meaning, encompassing a distinctive form of liturgy that evolved over the years, not to mention a cuisine and other cultural characteristics. They tended, as well, to be successful in trade and shipping, with a notable presence of wealthy families. The Sephardim came to represent one of the two great groupings of Judaism.

There is no apparent evidence of striving to be dominant, but it seemed a natural development for smaller groups, such as the Romaniotes, to share resources and to join Sephardi synagogues. To some extent this is what happened, too, in the case of the Mizrahim, which refers to those Jews who had originally made their homes in North Africa and in provinces in Western Asia, to the east of the homeland. But with the other major group of Jews formed through the diaspora, namely, the Ashkenazim, there was no such attempt to coalesce.

European Union

A map of where it all started, in the eastern Mediterranean, shows the most obvious land routes that would have been taken by those who saw their future further to the north. First, they would have passed through what is modern-day Lebanon and then northwards across Syria to Turkey. Roads charted by the Romans would have taken them to Constantinople and then, skirting the Black Sea, they could have followed one of two routes. One option was in a north-westwards direction, through the Balkans and on to the German states and the Low Countries; the other led directly north into Poland and, from there, some turned eastwards into Russia and Ukraine.

Even though it would have been tackled in stages, one can only imagine the hardships along the way. Groups of bedraggled travellers, offering to do laborious tasks in exchange for bread, searching for discarded vegetable peelings to make soup, children crying, old people struggling. From village to village, town to town, hot in summer, freezing in winter. But there was no going back. What started in tens became hundreds; hundreds became thousands; and over the centuries of the diaspora, thousands even turned into millions. For central and eastern Europe was where most Jews were to settle, at least until the Nazi Holocaust in just a few years destroyed a civilization that had taken root over millennia.

Hebrew was their language but, in order to communicate with the people they eventually lived amongst, a hybrid mainly of Hebrew and German evolved, known as Yiddish. Even for those who lived beyond the German states, Yiddish became the *lingua franca* to connect the dispersed Jewish communities across Europe. They held firmly to their original beliefs but, over a long period, it was inevitable that variations in practice crept in. When they were able to build their own synagogues, Jews in Holland or Poland would understand the liturgy but those who had never left the Mediterranean would have found some of it alien. A division widened between the two branches – the Sephardim and Ashkenazim – and although marriages between the two groups were by no means forbidden, they were not common.

The Ashkenazim were Europeans, their very name being derived from *Ashkenaz*, mediaeval Hebrew for Germany. Becoming established in their new lands was a long and faltering process, but from about 1000 CE their presence was well defined, especially in the west. Many made their home in the German states (well before they unified to become modern Germany), in spite of the fact that there were strict regulations on where they could settle. Especially punitive was their exclusion from the cities, leaving them to disperse amongst the smaller towns and villages. Conditions tended to be harsh and by the 13th century, there was a new phase of migration, this time eastwards to Poland, where, at least initially, they enjoyed greater freedom. There 'they filled an important economic role as a middle class between the feudal aristocracy and the peasants, and they managed most of the internal and foreign trade'.[15]

They prospered in Poland until, in the seventeenth century, they were victims of Cossack attacks from the east which led to mass killings. The Chmielncki massacres (named after the Cossack leader who wanted to see the eradication of all Jews in his territory) ended any sense of security for the Jews in Poland and encouraged a return to Germany. An important change was that now they were no longer denied settlement in some of the cities. They found new occupations and assimilated in other ways too, including some notable contributions to German culture. But always there was an incentive to find somewhere that would suit them better. Numbers kept increasing and more recent immigrants chose to go beyond Germany, into neighbouring Alsace (in eastern France), Amsterdam and (from the second half of the seventeenth century) to England.

Moss

Alsatian Pedigree

Although Alsace, in eastern France, was not immune from regular incidents of anti-Semitism and tight restrictions preventing them from living in cities, it seems that Jews have been present in the region from as early as 1000 CE. When Benjamin of Tudela visited Jewish communities across Europe in the twelfth century, he made a point of including Alsace on his itinerary.

The records of my own family fail to cover the whole of the period of Jewish settlement in Alsace but there is certainly evidence of a presence in the region (on the Moss side of the family) from as early as the eighteenth century. Jacob Nathan Moses was born in Alsace in 1722, although his father came originally from Holland. Jacob subsequently moved to London to trade as a hop merchant. His son, Samuel Eliezer Moses, almost certainly worked in the same trade and also lived in London for much of the time. He named one of his own sons, Wintzenheimer Moses, after a local village in Alsace with which he obviously had some connection, and he returned to that part of France later in his lifetime.

The Dutch link is also quite strong in this period and an earlier relative (also on grandmother Moss's side) was born in 1697 and known as Nathan Jacob Moses Segal of Rotterdam. His wife came from Hamburg but her family moved to Amsterdam early in the eighteenth century. The Dutch towns of Amersfoort and Leeuwarden also feature in the early records.

Perhaps of greater import, the family designation was changed from Moses to Moss at some point between 1817 and 1843. The latter date was when Jacob Nathan and his family moved from Amsterdam to Canada, by which time the children had all taken on the new name. Moses was just one of the strongly-Jewish names in my family that was consigned to history.

By the nineteenth century, an era of economic and cultural progress across much of Europe, one might have thought that the kind of uncertainties that surrounded the European Jews in earlier times would have passed. Far from it. Indeed, there were warning signs that could hardly be missed. Dark clouds were gathering, for instance, over western Russia where, from the end of the previous century as a result of the acquisition of Polish territory, the Russian state had become home to as many as five million Jews. That need not have been seen as a problem in itself but in the eyes of the Russian rulers it was, and a decision was taken to restrict their movement to a designated area known as the Pale of Settlement. Jews were not allowed to move beyond the Pale and they were hemmed in, as well, by other restrictions.

Elsewhere, too, the hatred that had poisoned relations over previous centuries had certainly not dissipated and Jews once again found themselves subjected to a series of vicious attacks on their lives and property. A new word, of Slavic derivation, entered the English language – the *pogrom* – to describe the organized massacre of Jews in eastern Europe and western Russia (where some of these events were incited directly by the state). The pogroms were as devastating as any form of persecution in the past, and the turn of the century saw a mass migration away from eastern Europe. Although it must have seemed like another step into the dark, a majority took the opportunity buy tickets to cross the Atlantic where they could find new homes in the United States and also Canada and South America. As well as fleeing for their immediate safety, the prospect of a better material life was, in any case, an important inducement to move from Europe.

Some two million Jews left Russia alone between 1880 and 1920 and they were joined by large numbers from Poland and Germany. They travelled from the east in crowded trains, sometimes in locked carriages to keep them apart from other passengers, with many of them alighting at Bremen where they waited for an onward boat; more than three million left from the twin ports of Bremen/Bremerhaven in the peak period of emigration, leading up to the Second World War.[16] Tragically, many stayed on the mainland of Europe, especially in Poland and Germany, perhaps hoping in vain for better times, only to face mass execution in the next few years. Jews constantly live in hope that anti-Semitism has had its day but, time and again, such optimism is badly misplaced.

This period saw the diaspora at its height, with Jews migrating to a variety of destinations to escape further persecution. As we will see in the following chapter, many of my own family had already chosen England as their new home. Given what happened to Jewish families who remained on the continent, it proved to be a wise (although, in most cases, probably unintended) choice with enormous consequences.

Chapter 2

The Shores of Albion

Most of my direct descendants came to England in the second half of the
nineteenth and early twentieth centuries, along with other Jewish families
at that time who were also seeking to escape the mounting persecution
in continental Europe. They were not deterred by the earlier experience
of their forebears in this island nation, in which the original Jewish
community was cruelly treated and subsequently evicted in its entirety.
To allay any fears this time, they would have been pleased to discover
that, by the time they arrived, some Jewish families (including a number
of their own distant relatives) were already living here and able to get on
peacefully with their lives. For the newcomers, there was hope that they
could do the same.

Albion Beckons

*Albion… the earliest-known name for the island of Britain. It was used by
ancient Greek geographers from the 4th century BC and even earlier.*[17]

It had all started well enough, with Jews (who came largely from France)
settling in this country towards the end of the eleventh century, in the
wake of William the Conqueror and with the expectation of an era of
peace and prosperity. The prospect of freedom as well as an assured income
in a growing economy was probably too much to hope for, as they soon
discovered that their settlement was conditional on undertaking the work
of moneylenders.[18] For that occupation, they already had an established
reputation and William was quick to see the importance of efficient
moneylending for the development of trade, not to mention a source of
revenue for the royal coffers. This was not the peripheral occupation it
was later to become, after banks took over the main business of lending,
and trade at that time could not manage without a small group of
experienced 'usurers' (those who were allowed to charge interest for their
loans). Unfortunately, no matter how important it was to the wealth of the
nation, the much-despised practice of usury continued to attract bitter
opposition (the interest charged on loans invariably believed by borrowers

to be too high). As a result, Jews were commonly reviled, simply for doing the job they were assigned.

Their vulnerability as an alien group was increased by the fact that they had to live in small communities around the country, oiling the wheels of commerce wherever it took place. At one time there were as many as 16,000 Jews living in England but they were widely dispersed. They found homes in scattered market towns like York and Lincoln, Norwich and Bristol, a foreign-looking minority with their own language, stared at by adults and mocked by children. It was a tenuous existence and, sure enough, it ended unhappily when, just two centuries after their arrival, they were cast out of the country which they had hoped would become their permanent home.[19]

The expulsion took place in 1290 by order of the then monarch, Edward I, but hostility towards the Jews had been simmering almost from the time of their arrival. It hardly helped that the two centuries of their settlement in England coincided with the early Crusades, when Jews were seen as no better than the hated Saracens, both treated as enemies of Christ. Successive monarchs, unwilling to lose valuable income, had offered protection for the beleaguered Jewish communities but this meant little in the face of bitter opposition from neighbouring barons and burgesses. Persecution took place on a regular basis, sometimes at a very localized level but also erupting at times into riots and even massacres. Once again, the Jews were forced to pack up and go in search of somewhere safer.

For the next 400 years, Jews were forbidden entry to England, only to be allowed back in the seventeenth century when Oliver Cromwell, the Lord Protector and victor of the English Civil War, opened the gates once more. At first there was no great rush to return, until the intensification of pogroms in the German states and countries to the east led, two centuries later, to new waves of incomers. When they arrived, they were overwhelmingly poor and had no guarantee that their welcome would be any more enduring than the last time Jews settled in England, but at least they would leave behind the constant threat of vilification and mass killings. Once again, a new start beckoned.

There were pressing issues for the newly arrived – at the most practical level, simply finding a place to live and work so they could earn enough to feed their families. But in quieter moments, for those who arrived in the middle of the nineteenth century, it would not have escaped their notice that they had come to a country with a renowned politician (who would later become prime minister) by the name of Benjamin Disraeli. Never mind that he came from a Jewish family of non-believers and as a young boy had been baptized as an Anglian. Never mind, too, that the adult Disraeli was a Victorian dandy who thought nothing of dressing in immaculate suits adorned with brightly coloured silks. His was a world apart from the ragged, dowdy individuals who came off the boats with their few belongings over their shoulders. But what a name! How could it be that anyone who sounded so Jewish had attained such an esteemed position in society? And in England of all places, at the very heart of a great empire. For the unknowing, it must almost have seemed that they were stepping foot on the very shores of Zion.

Off the boats came many of my ancestors, people like Moses Moses and Moses Lazarus, Jacob Joseph and Joseph Joseph, Abraham Shashoua and Abraham Abrahams. Biblical names with an oriental twist. If someone called Benjamin Disraeli could make it in English society, surely there was hope for them all. They need not even change their names. If they investigated further they would have discovered, too, that a select group of earlier immigrants had by then gained access to the higher echelons of society. Most notably, the Rothchilds had retained their religion while at the same time winning social acceptance, not to mention owning grandiose properties in the English countryside (hitherto the unquestioned preserve of the aristocracy).[20]

England was a welcoming environment in other ways too, with a progressive loosening of restrictions on its Jewish population. But there was still more to be done. It was generally overlooked that the highest office of state would have been barred to Disraeli had he not previously rejected his religion of birth. However, well before the end of the century, even that restriction had been lifted and their emancipation was largely complete. Jews in this second wave of settlement were even able to own land in this blessed country. Now it was up to them alone to find a niche where they could prosper in their chosen ways.

But they were not unrealistic. Their experience of persecution was engrained and even the most idealistic amongst them would not have expected anything more than a tacit acceptance of their arrival. That, after all, was all that they asked for and that, more or less, was what they received. Not entirely, perhaps, as there were to be repeated instances of anti-Semitism, but nothing like the untamed violence and threats to their very existence that they had suffered on the continent – and would have continued to do so had they remained. This time they had found a liberal society where a number of esteemed individuals were willing to speak up for them, so that it was not only the voices of their enemies that could be heard.

Unlike their first encounter with England in the eleventh century, when they had to disperse to find work, this time they tended to concentrate in large cities. Most made their way to one of two destinations – London and Manchester (again, in coherent communities) – with smaller clusters in other cities like Leeds, Liverpool and Glasgow. And in creating these concentrations they shared a common characteristic that is typical of new arrivals in a country, seeking the company of fellow exiles with the same beliefs and customs, sometimes even coming from the same faraway village. Their previous circumstances had often forced them into small but tight-knit communities, or ghettoes, and, even though they were no longer forced to do so, it would have seemed only natural to continue to live close to other Jews.

East Enders

Into the heart of east London they came… streams of Jewish exiles, refugees, settlers, few as well-to-do as the Jew of the proverb, but all rich in their cheerfulness, their industry, and their cleverness. The majority bore with them nothing but their phylacteries and praying shawls.[21]

East London (or, more particularly, the area usually known as the East End) absorbed most of the incoming Jews in this period. Some arrived even before the eighteenth century, and by 1850 'the ghetto was firmly established around the focal point of Petticoat Lane' and in the narrow alleyways and dank buildings to the east.[22] But it was from around 1880 and into the new century that most disembarked in the London docks and found their way through the dingy streets to their future homes. Word of mouth drew them to locations where there might still be the odd room (or even part of a room) in overcrowded tenements. As many as 120,000 arrived at that time from Russia and Poland, with a further 20,000 from Germany, Holland, Austria and Romania.[23]

The main waves of immigration stemmed directly from the worst instances of the pogroms in western Russia and central and eastern Europe. Although the Nazi Holocaust was still some years away, already across the continent there were ominous signs of growing intolerance. In the beleaguered communities in these countries, England was spoken of as a place of salvation, although little would have been known about the conditions they would find. The fact is that space was already at a premium in the traditional district bounded by Spitalfields, Commercial Street and Whitechapel. With expansion to the west barred by the boundaries of the City of London, for extra space they were forced to look further east.[24] Street by street, they pressed their way outwards, taking in the southern fringes of Bethnal Green, and on to Stepney and the more distant Mile End. Today, these districts are the names of underground stations on the Central Line and it is sobering to imagine how, along the streets above, some of our forebears once trundled carts filled with their worldly belongings, searching for a place where they could start their new lives.

Most of the newcomers were desperately poor, and living conditions were sub-standard in every way. Yet, somehow, they also managed to squeeze into this warren of activity additional workshops to carry on a trade, home-based synagogues so they could pray together, and tiny stores where they could buy the kind of food they had known before.[25] It was a world within a world, and the perceptive social investigator, Charles Booth, observed that 'they live and crowd together and work and meet their fate independent of the great stream of London life surging around them'.[26] They looked inwards but depended on the tolerance of the society beyond.

Social commentators at the time and since have portrayed the area as one of great deprivation, a maze of alleys and staircases leading to hopelessly overcrowded homes and workshops where sewing machines turned night and day to ensure survival in the highly competitive environment. In some ways, the most sentient account of what it was like came from Israel Zangwill, a talented writer who grew up within the community and did more than simply measure the size of rooms and the number of hours worked. Born in London in 1864, his parents had come to England from eastern Europe, seemingly just another family seeking refuge. Exceptionally for that period, however, Israel gained entry to the University of London and emerged with an honours degree in English, French and Mental & Moral Science. He was a prodigious writer but the work which best captures the spirit of the Jewish community at the time was first published in 1892, when the main flow of immigrants was arriving. His book, *Children of the Ghetto: A study of a peculiar people*, gets to the very heart of community life and vividly brings to mind a Dickensian caricature. He tells of the pinched lives of people largely hidden behind dusty shopfronts and in the tiny rooms above, the sun seldom seen but their lives lightened with a keen sense of humour and interspersed with a rich tradition of Yiddish words and phrases.

Zangwill misses nothing, treating the reader to an assortment of sometimes hilarious stories of celebration and religious observance, of family landmarks and romance which could hardly stay hidden at such close quarters. To take just one example, there is the account of Silverman's bar mitzvah, when the boy of the hour, young Ebenezer, does all that is asked of him while some of the men indulge in slipping tasty morsels into their pockets to take home. Mrs Silverman, like a good Jewish housewife, lays out some biscuits and fruit 'not appertaining to the meal, but provided for the refreshment of the less-favored visitors – such as Mr. and Mrs. Hyams – who would be dropping in during the day'. For the more favoured, there was a meal to be enjoyed, starting, of course, with the mandatory fried fish. 'Excellent fish… first-class plaice, Mrs Silverman' were the expected compliments from fortunate guests before everyone helped themselves.

Amidst the eternal banter there was one guest who sat quietly, lost in his own thoughts. No-one in the ghetto knew much about Joseph Strelitski as he spent his time buried in his books but it was known that as a boy he had lived in Siberia. Money seemed not to matter for him and… 'in the streets he walked with tight-pursed lips, dreaming no one knew what'.

And yet there were times when his tight-pursed lips unclenched themselves and he drew in great breaths even of Ghetto air with the huge contentment of one who has known suffocation. "One can breathe here," he seemed to be saying. The atmosphere, untainted by spies, venal officials, and jeering soldiery, seemed fresh and sweet. Here the ground was stable, not mined in all directions; no arbitrary 'ukase' – veritable sword of Damocles – hung over the head and darkened the sunshine. In such a country, where faith was free and action untrammelled, mere living was an ecstasy when remembrance came over one, and so Joseph Strelitski sometimes threw back his head and breathed in liberty. The voluptuousness of the sensation cannot be known by born freemen.[27]

For all the jousting and arguments, humour and laughter, pathos – as Joseph Strelitski reminds us – was never far beneath the surface. Jews will surely recognize this compendium of experience and sometimes conflicting emotions as an enduring trait.

Nor, in spite of the good times, is the shadow of anti-Semitism far away: relations between communities in the East End were immeasurably better than most of them had known before, but it was by no means absent. Theirs, after all, was 'a society within a society' and not immune from the kind of prejudice that seemed to follow Jews everywhere. Perhaps, predictably, the more they displaced previous groups and established their own identity, the more they faced the kind of hostility that invariably confronts new waves of migrants. There was widespread resentment and indiscriminate blame was directed to the aliens for everything from taking jobs and housing to the certainty that it must have been a Jew behind the murders in that area attributed to the notorious Jack the Ripper. It is a familiar argument that immigrants increase the supply of labour and reduce the level of wages, so it was not surprising that some of the fiercest opposition came from fellow workers competing for what little there was. Foremost amongst their accusers were trade unionists like Ben Tillett (himself from an Irish immigrant family), who was not reluctant to fan the flames of prejudice among his union membership of dockworkers:

> ... *the influx of continental pauperism aggravates and multiplies the number of ills which press so heavily upon us... Foreigners come to London in large numbers, herd together in habitations unfit for beasts, the sweating system allowing the more grasping and shrewd a life of comparative ease in superintending the work.*[28]

It helped to cool the temperature that the wave of immigration was not unending and, by the time that the First World War was declared, the number of Jews in the East End had already passed its peak. This was partly because the influx had slowed (a result very largely of regulations introduced to restrict the flow) but also because one could already see the start of an outward movement to less congested parts of London. By sheer hard work, and perhaps a modicum of good fortune, tailors and shopkeepers, rag traders and jewellery craftsmen, furniture finishers and lace-makers, accumulated just enough to move out of the most deprived areas. Some chose to move further east, following the main roads and railway lines to places like Ilford and later Gants Hill. Others went north, with an important community of orthodox Jews establishing itself in Stamford Hill, or north-westwards to new suburbs that, in their greenery, must have seemed a world apart. Often it was not a single move but one made in stages, perhaps to inner city destinations like Hackney and Clapton in the first instance, and later to the most popular venue of all, Golders Green. Arrive there, at the foot of Hampstead Heath, and the world could see that you'd made it; it is hard even to say the name, Golders Green, without succumbing to a Yiddish inflexion.

My own ancestors have their personal stories to tell of how they left the traditional neighbourhoods in east London, in favour of more salubrious surroundings. The family of my paternal grandmother, Julia Goodman, born in the heart of the Jewish community in the East End, must have been typical of others at the time who made their own way to what were seen as better parts of London.

Goodman/Hardy

Coming out of the East End

In the Essex suburbs, older people still speak of how they 'came out of the East End', seeing it as a social rather than just a geographical journey. The path of Julia Goodman was a case in question.

The evidence suggests that Julia's father, Joseph, came originally from Austria, but her mother, Sarah Abrahams, was already living in the flourishing community of immigrant Jews in the East End. In fact, Sarah came from a long line of tailors in the area, and grew up in a street where her parents' neighbours included a hawker and a tailor, a bedstead maker and a locksmith, a cigar maker and someone who made needles. It would have been colourful and noisy, a busy place of enterprise with no room for anyone who thought they could get away with doing nothing.

Julia herself was born in the East End, but soon moved, with her parents, to one of the newly-developed suburbs in north-west London. It was there that she met Hardy Simon (known in the family as Sam), the man she was to marry. Sam's father, Max, had previously brought his family from Germany, with enough money, as a result of his previous piano-making business in Hanover, to 'leapfrog' the more common starting point of the East End and move direct to the new suburb.

One can see why they would want to leave the East End. After the initial feeling of relief at arriving safely from continental Europe, the congested conditions they then found themselves in would have encouraged thoughts of how to move somewhere better. Circumstances, however, were never the same from one family to another, and sometimes it would be the most unlikely reasons that led to a new beginning. One might have thought that being convicted of what seem now to be petty crimes and then transported from London to the far side of the world would hardly lead to good fortune, but for two related families that is exactly what happened. Their exceptional story is told in a later chapter, on a further stage in the diaspora.

'And May He Live in Manchester'

The Sephardi merchant elite already possessed sophisticated trading networks based largely on family connections which had been operating for centuries in the Mediterranean and the Middle East. It was inevitable that before long they too would be drawn to the city by the opportunities to trade.[29]

While all that was going on in the East End, 180 miles north-west of London, some of the incoming Jews were drawn, instead, to the industrial and commercial city of Manchester. Such was the lure of this provincial capital that when Jewish boys in the Levant were squealing at the approach of the rabbi's circumcision knife, it is said that family onlookers would mutter the words 'and may he live in Manchester'.[30] Probably, at that crucial moment, an infant son would have chosen to live anywhere but on the dining-room table where his ordeal was taking place. Later, as he grew up, the metropolis famed for being at the heart of the cotton industry might not have seemed such a bad idea.

Manchester occupies a special place in Jewish history in England, not least of all for some of the families that have inspired this book. Like east London, most of the early incomers were Ashkenazi families, with Sephardi Jews just a small proportion of the total. But small though they were in number, the Sephardim had a disproportionate influence on the commercial life of the city. They brought with them – from the Eastern Mediterranean and Iraq – their own valuable connections in the cotton trade, as well as associated interests in merchant shipping and shipbuilding. And they generally fared well as a result, in time living in spacious houses with domestic staff, and meeting for business or socializing in the prestigious Midland Hotel and in their own synagogue communities.

Earlier, in the 1750s, when the first Jews arrived in Manchester they tended to engage in transient occupations, sometimes as hawkers and pedlars trading second-hand goods (known dismissively as 'slops'). Alternatively, some brought with them skills from their former countries, with experience of working with jewellery, clocks and watches or an expertise in engraving and calligraphy. There is not much evidence of Sephardic influence in the busy Jewish community until after 1840, when the cotton industry lured migrants from places like Gibraltar and Constantinople. The 1841 Census shows that 76 Jews were then engaged in one aspect or another of the cotton trade, a number which was soon to rise. In spite of business connections with Aleppo, it was not until 1843 that the first Syrian came with a view to settling permanently in Manchester.[31] It was not uncommon for a father to come first on a temporary basis, living in lodgings while he developed links locally and tested the market, before committing to a permanent move with the rest of his family. Exchanging the blue skies and gentle rhythms of the Mediterranean for the perennial drizzle and smoky grime of Manchester was not a decision to be taken lightly.

Over the next few decades, a growing (though still quite modest) number of Sephardi families appeared in the records, a total of 39 households by 1871. What is interesting is how many of these newcomers had followed the same path to Manchester, with the largest single number coming from Corfu (and often before that from Arta). Corfu remained a British protectorate until 1864, at which point it was ceded to Greece. Not surprisingly, it was believed that applicants for British citizenship stood a better chance of success if they could demonstrate good standing when they were under British jurisdiction, than if they had been living in newly independent Greece or elsewhere in the wider Ottoman empire.

Abdela

Constantinople, Athens and London

Jacob Elia Abdela (my great grandfather) was one such applicant who stood to gain from the situation. He prepared the ground for his application while he was still in Corfu and the records show that he lived for five years in Manchester before he was successful in being awarded British citizenship. It would not have gone unnoticed that Jacob Elia was of high standing and had taken an active part in the public affairs of the island. He had for eight years been President of the Greek Jewish Synagogue in Corfu and during that time he received King George of Greece on his official visit to the island.

The key document in the process to become a British citizen was a 'Certificate of Naturalization to an Alien', issued by the Home Office in London. One such certificate, numbered 2742, was issued to Jacob Elia Abdela, who was then living at 16 Broughton Street, Cheetham Hill Road in North Manchester. It was stated that the applicant was a subject of the Empire of Turkey. He was at the time of his application forty years old, registered as a merchant and with three children born in Corfu (Suvi, Elia and Isaac). In the previous eight years, for five of these he had been a resident of the United Kingdom and, if naturalized, intended to remain there.

Anyone who has sought entry to a foreign country will know the relief felt when the immigration official, having inspected one's passport, eventually lifts a stamp on the counter and brings it down with a thud onto the respective form.

Now in pursuance of the authority given to me in the said Acts, I grant to the aforesaid, Jacob Elia Abdela, this Certificate and declare that he is a British Subject.

The date was the 26th October 1878.

An interesting condition in the coveted certificate was that if someone was naturalized British but later chose to return to the country where they were previously a citizen, then their British citizenship would not apply for the duration of the visit. This caveat had special meaning when, some years later, in 1905, one of the sons, Elia Abdela, having moved to Constantinople, wished to confirm his continuing right to British protection. It was clearly a matter of concern to him that his status be clarified and his lawyer produced a detailed argument to show why his client should receive special protection. His case rested on whether it could be shown that Elia (whose father was born in Arta) was not also a citizen of the Ottoman Empire.

Abdela

Navigating the International Chessboard

Elia was the second son of Jacob Elia Abdela. He was born in Corfu in 1870 and grew up in Manchester. At some point he moved for business reasons to Constantinople, where in 1901 he married Hélène Crisafulli.

But there must have been a question about his status and he commissioned a lawyer to confirm with the British Consul in Constantinople that he should continue to enjoy British protection. The submission all hinged on when the town of Arta, where his father was born, was formally ceded to Greece. An international treaty was invoked to make the case. Until he was naturalized British, Elia was previously a Turkish citizen but had that since been revoked?

Until Arta became part of Greece, it was still within the Ottoman Empire and, therefore, Elia's father was previously Turkish. His father's naturalization as a British citizen – and with that, the rest of his family – came three years before Arta was ceded to Greece. In other words, for the first few years of his life, young Elia remained a citizen of the Ottoman Empire but then (through his father's naturalization) he became British.

With Arta in 1881 becoming part of the modern nation state of Greece, everything changed. Under international treaty, citizens of Arta could apply to remain Turkish but they were only given three years to do so. As Elia did not apply to do so, his previous status was now confirmed as Greek.

This meant that he could live in Turkey and continue to enjoy British protection. Only if he had still been Turkish would there have been a question over this, but that was no longer in dispute.

It is interesting to note that the lawyer who wrote on behalf Elia added a handwritten note at the top of his letter, saying that he had chosen to meet the British Consul to make the case in person. He concludes that the Consul agreed with what he said.

The first point of arrival for most of the Sephardim when they came to England was in the Cheetham Hill district of Manchester, to the north of the city centre. There was already a flourishing Ashkenazi community there and, until their numbers grew, the smaller number of Sephardim were invited to use the Ashkenazi Great Synagogue for their marriage and burial needs. Ashkenazim and Sephardim alike were all Jewish but the two traditions each had their own way of doing things, not only at prayer but also on ceremonial occasions. Within a short time, though, to meet the direct needs of the Sephardi community, the foundation stone was laid for the construction of their own Spanish and Portuguese Synagogue in Cheetham Hill, followed some years later by the purchase of land for a separate cemetery.

Yet, even while they were consolidating their position in the northern suburb, individual Sephardi families were choosing to move to less developed areas in south Manchester, especially Withington and Didsbury (adjoining districts, some four to five miles from the city centre). Summarizing the situation, the biographer of the Sephardi community in Manchester, Lydia Collins, concludes that:

> By the outbreak of World War I there were over a hundred Sephardi families in Manchester. By now the centre of gravity was shifting and south Manchester became the driving force of the community although the north Manchester congregation continued and some of the older families never moved south.[32]

Over the previous half century or so, the most successful business leaders had steadily accumulated small (or not so small) fortunes for their families. The clearest evidence of this came in their ability to finance the upkeep of large, newly-built houses in the southern suburbs. Two roads were especially favoured, Palatine and Clyde, which ran in parallel from north to south and where the size of houses typically ranged from twelve rooms and upwards, more than enough not only for the families themselves but also for domestic staff.

Abdela/Moss

Sephardi Neighbours

Sophia Abdela, better known as 'Birdie', was my maternal grandmother. She grew up in London and, when she married Isaac Abdela in 1903, she went to live in Manchester. Isaac was by then well established in shipping and they moved into 79 Palatine Road, a 12-roomed property considered large enough to bring up their three children. With her own staff including a sick nurse, a domestic nurse, a cook and a housemaid, Birdie was spared the domestic chores.

Along the same road, at number 53, was Birdie's sister, Rosalind, married to Setton Nessim Menache (also known as Nessim Abraham Meanasce). Theirs was a 15-room house, with two servants, but in 1912 her husband died and she had to move. Isaac's sister, Rachel, is later recorded as living, with her Baghdadian husband Joseph Shasha, at number 120. Meanwhile, in nearby Clyde Road, Isaac Abdela's brother, Suvi, resided with his wife, Dora, in another spacious property. Domestic staff lived in, but there were no children to fill the empty rooms. Later they moved to Monte Carlo.

Palatine Road was clearly the place for aspiring families to be, a local bastion of wealth and respectability. Other residents in the road included doctors, dentists, merchants, businessmen and people of private means. The Abdelas would also have felt at home amongst neighbours from overseas, a number of whom were clearly Jewish. At number 23, for instance, were the Levys, who came originally from Janina in Turkey and whose son was born in Corfu. Two houses down from Isaac and Birdie, there was Isaac Judah Isaac, from Baghdad, who also had a shipping business in Manchester.

With the progressive shift of Sephardi families to the south of the city, it is not surprising that attention soon turned to providing a new synagogue to serve the community. As early as 1903, a property was bought in the neighbouring district of Withington, and converted over the following year into a place of worship. Before long, that, too, could barely cope with the growing numbers in its catchment. Nor was it just a question of numbers, as there was also a demand for somewhere to meet the specific needs of the Syrians and Baghdadians, who both had difficulties with the Spanish and Portuguese rituals at the existing synagogue. As a result, a property was bought for the latter group in, of all places, Palatine Road – at the very hub of Sephardi life – and the first services were held in 1919. Two sizeable synagogues in the same district, however, proved a step too far and once again a single venue was proposed, this time an impressive, purpose-built construction. Even then, not everyone was satisfied and about half the congregation in Palatine Road opted, instead, for their own, smaller place of worship, the Shaare Sedek Synagogue.

Religious practice and the rituals associated with births and deaths were essential to the life of the community but so, too, were social activities. A small tennis club was opened before 1914, and a photograph shows an even number of men and women, all meeting the standards of an obvious dress code. There was also a literary and social society, organized under the auspices of the synagogue, with a wide range of activities for Sephardim of all ages. But the biggest change came in 1922, with the opening of the Manchester Country Club. This is where the community gathered for a variety of leisure activities, including popular dances and card parties. When the land had to be sold to keep it financially afloat, the club moved to a house in Palatine Road. The area was also well-served by two prestigious grammar schools, Manchester Grammar School for boys and the similarly well-regarded Withington Girls' School. While the children met non-Jewish peers, their parents, however:

> *rarely socialised outside the Jewish circle. Most of their recreational time was spent involved with charity work, literary and dramatic societies and concerts, particularly for the interest of the Jewish community's youngsters.*[33]

Manchester's Sephardi Jews had come a long way since they were drawn to one of the great industrial workshops of the world. Money was made in the business districts of the city and then invested in the palatial residences of the southern suburbs. A survey at the time suggested that by 1930 'a third of the houses in Palatine Road and Clyde Road were occupied by Sephardi families, and that these two roads alone accounted for 40% of Sephardi settlement in south Manchester'.[34] So it was in this area that they carved out a community with everything they wanted – synagogue and burial ground, country club, substantial homes with well-tended gardens. In the opulent environment they created, was there perhaps a hint of what they had previously known in Beirut or Alexandria? In the country club was this a forerunner of what became so popular in upstate New York in the 1950s, a place where Jews could feel safe and mix with their own people without calls for them to be barred?

But, as every Jew knows through experience, nothing lasts forever. The 1920s was not the best time for business, and that was before the Wall Street Crash of 1929 unleashed the Great Depression that cut through the whole of the world economy. No activity or area was immune and Manchester's cotton and shipping industries were certainly no exception. The hitherto unquestionable power of King Cotton was no more.

Even if they avoided a total collapse, established businesses in these sectors were forced to make changes. Old certainties disappeared overnight. The world was changing and the pillars which supported the comfortable life of south Manchester were no longer stable. In time, the spacious houses would be subdivided into flats, or converted for professional offices or institutional use. Many Jews remained in the area but it would never again be what it was.

Chapter 3

The Diaspora... Again

One might have thought, after all they had been through, that finding a home in England would have been enough. It was surely time to put down roots. Anti-Semitism in their new homeland was by no means absent (taking the form more of latent prejudice than an immediate threat of violence) but there was, at least, the blessing that life could evolve with a reasonable degree of normality. And for a majority this was, indeed, all that was wanted. But this is ignoring the fact that 'moving on' is in the bloodstream. More than two millennia of rootlessness takes its toll. For an aspiring Jew, there would always be a new frontier to cross. If *not* the Promised Land ahead, then at least another land of promise.

In this chapter we tell of families who first settled in England but then, for one reason or another – and the reasons were, indeed, very different – moved on again. This time they set their sights, not on established countries in Europe, but on different parts of the New World. In all cases they were drawn by fresh opportunities that awaited, on distant continents – Australasia, Africa, and America (North and South). The second diaspora was not like the first, fuelled by the sounds of armies to the rear, forcing them out of lands they had previously inhabited. Nor were belongings packed in a rush to escape the ferocity of the pogroms. But in their own way the new journeys were no less difficult, requiring fortitude as well as imagination to make the decision to leave one's place of refuge in order to seek somewhere that might be better. At least by then, the whole business of putting down fresh roots was well versed. Jews of all people were practiced in the art.

Intrepid Travellers

In calm weather a sailing ship might take as long as four months, while a well-run clipper ship with favourable winds could make the journey in a little over half this time.[35]

There are some exotic tales in the records but none more so than the incredible achievements of two related families, the Nathans and the

Josephs (who were ancestors of the Moss side of the family). Their interlinked stories stretch the very bounds of credulity, with all the ingredients of a fictional best-seller. And the common thread that holds the various episodes together is their willingness to endure the long and dangerous sea voyage to Australia and New Zealand, and the harsh conditions on arrival, where they saw, quite rightly, great opportunities awaiting.

The challenge of surviving the long voyage from the Port of London to one of the few Australian ports at the time, and in some cases transferring to a smaller boat for the remainder of the journey across the notorious Tasman Sea to New Zealand, cannot be overstated. Especially in the days of sail, in the first half of the nineteenth century, everything about it was intimidating. Several months at sea – living in cramped and rudimentary quarters where infection was prone to spread between passengers, through some of the roughest seas on the planet where the threat of a shipwreck was never far away – was a venture not to be taken lightly. Only the most intrepid (or those forced to do so) would have embarked on such an adventure.

Some, of course, had no choice, being ordered to leave the country by the courts. Transportation was a punishment to be feared. From the last quarter of the eighteenth century until the middle of the next, the courts saw in transportation an opportunity to relieve pressures on overcrowded prisons in Britain, as well as providing free labour to develop the new colonies on the other side of the world.

By current standards, the threshold of conviction was low and, at least in theory, the price high. Those penalized in this way were summarily remanded to await the next convict ship bound for one of the penal colonies ready to receive them. If they survived the journey, convicts were assigned on arrival to hard labour, living as well as working in conditions that were severe in the extreme. Depending on the gravity of their crime, they remained in servitude for an allotted period of time, sometimes for life. Those who completed a fixed sentence, then had the choice either to stay in Australia or return to Britain. There were less exacting ways to leave the squalid conditions of the East End – but in the examples which follow it proved to be a blessing in disguise.

Nathan Lyon Nathan

The young man who started an extraordinary sequence of events was Nathan Lyon Nathan. Or at least that was how he was generally known; for some reason, at different times, he used a number of aliases including Nathan Nathan or Nathaniel Newton.

Moss

A Voyage to a Dynasty

Nathan Lyon Nathan was born in Spitalfields, east London in 1783. His father, Judah, came from Holland but little is known about his mother. He is an ancestor of mine on the Moss side of the family, that can be traced back through the lineage of my grandmother, née Birdie Moss. At the age of sixteen, Nathan was convicted and tried at the Old Bailey for 'grand larceny', his crime being to steal the following items: a silk handkerchief, value 1d.; a gown, value 2s. 6d.; a stannel petticoat, value 3s.; a calico petticoat, value 4s.; a shift, value 2s. 6d.; a pair of stockings, value 2s.; an apron, value 1s. 6d.; a half-shawl, value 2s.; two half-handkerchiefs, value 6d.; four caps, value 2s.; and two pocket-handkerchiefs, value 1s. The total value of all of the items came to little more than one pound in 'old money'.[36]

He was found guilty by the court and held in custody until a place could be found for him on a convict ship bound for New South Wales. After a wait of three months, he was taken from prison to board 'The Royal Admiral' on one of the first shipments to Australia. When he disembarked on 20 November 1800, he was barely seventeen years of age. The period of Nathan's sentence was seven years, after which he had the option of staying in Australia or returning to England. He chose the latter.

One might have thought the experience would have so demoralized the young man that he could well have returned with bitterness in his heart and a life of petty crime ahead of him. But it had just the opposite effect. By the time Nathan returned to London he was still young and he lost no time in getting married. His wife, Sarah, also had the name of Nathan and her family, too, came from Holland. Her father, Hyam Chaim, was possibly a tailor, living and working in Whitechapel.

(...cont'd)

As if to make up for lost time, Nathan and Sarah parented a large family of nine children, all of whom he would later encourage to migrate to one of the Australian colonies or New Zealand. Not in shackles this time, like their father, but as free men and women eager to make new lives for themselves.[37] Clearly, for Nathan, the Antipodes was the place to be, offering opportunities not available in England. He had seen for himself how much could be done, bringing in and selling essential supplies and building new townships. His enthusiasm was infectious and, as we will see later, all of his nine sons and daughters prospered as a result.

Morse Moses Joseph

The other central character in the making of the dynasty had, in some ways, an even more remarkable story to tell. Born Morse Moses Joseph, he preferred to be known simply as Moses Joseph.

Moss

Moses in Exile

Like the story of Nathan Lyon Nathan, this one also begins in the congested streets of east London. Born in 1803, Moses Joseph worked in a small tobacco store in Whitechapel. At the age of 23, he was found guilty of stealing a watch 'or some other piece of jewellery' from a fellow trader; there was also a suggestion in one report that he was handling counterfeit money, a more likely offence as he was duly sentenced to transportation for life and sent to the still sparsely populated colony of New South Wales.

On boarding the convict ship, the 'Albion', Moses was following closely in the footsteps of Nathan Lyon Nathan, the man who would become his future father-in-law. Nor was he the first from the local Jewish community to make this journey; the seven convict ships of the First Fleet in 1788, for instance, recorded on its passenger list no fewer than twelve Jewish offenders.

There is no knowing how he fared on the long voyage, but one of his descendants puts a very unlikely gloss on the experience. It sounds more as if, at the end of the voyage, the young man had just emerged from a leisurely cruise: 'he arrived in Sydney Town on 20 May 1827, well rested, fit, literate and vigorous – just the assets needed to help him on his way'. Descriptions of what it was really like for convicts tell a very different story and, in the course of their arduous voyage, most would hardly have expected to see land again.

We can only speculate how Moses viewed the prospect of a life in exile, not least of all because he was already pledged to marry his first cousin, Rosetta Nathan (one of the many offspring of Nathan and Sarah). His passion was undimmed by the long journey and he soon wrote to Rosetta, asking her to join him in the Australian colony. He was still a convict, with a lifetime of servitude ahead, and living half a world away from the tight-knit community where his family remained. One could have understood if young Rosetta had declined the invitation but (like her father and Moses himself) she was made of sterner stuff. It is also no coincidence that her father, with first-hand experience of the colony, could only speak well of what it had to offer. As a result of a combination of romance and paternal advice, Rosetta duly booked a ticket on the 'Margaret' and arrived in Sydney in 1832. Her marriage to Moses took place in the same year.

Like his father-in-law, Moses had chosen a tortuous way to leave the East End but the real drama of his life was yet to come. In the following chapter, on Jewish businesses, we will see how Moses came into his own, revealing unique skills as well as fortitude to make a great success of his future in the new colony. Indeed, Moses and Rosetta were to prove a truly formidable couple, and the contribution of Rosetta is separately assessed in a later chapter on Jewish women.

Nathan Lyon Nathan and his son-in-law, Moses Joseph, were both to have large families and their offspring prospered in the same way as their parents.

Nathan's Family

In the case of the Nathans, their children were born in England so they had to make a conscious choice to travel to the colonies (to New Zealand as well as Australia) – which they all did.

Moss

Surely the Promised Land

Apart from Rosetta (who was the oldest of the nine Nathan children), the other eight brothers and sisters *all* went either to Australia or New Zealand to build their careers. It is a remarkable record and it is highly unlikely that this would have happened if their father had not been transported for seven years in the first place.

Louis and his wife Harriette found their way to Hobart, Tasmania, making a great success in business and returning to England in 1842, when Louis was by then (after only eight years) a rich man.

Rachel left England as a single woman but soon married Samuel Cohen at Port Macquarie in New South Wales. She returned to England when her husband died in 1861.

Arthur made the journey to Australia before he was thirty and married Caroline Cohen. They had children and lived for most of the time in Tasmania but, like others in the family, came back to settle in England.

David had an illustrious career, starting with his arrival in Sydney on the 'Orient' in 1839, and his decision to continue to New Zealand aboard the 'Achilles'. Two years later, in the first Jewish service held in New Zealand, he married a widow, Rosetta Aarons (née Jacobs). The couple returned to England for a while but New Zealand was by then their real home. Rosetta died there in 1864 and David remarried, this time to Edith Barrow Montefiore. His own death, in Auckland, occurred in 1886.

Burnett Baruch was born and died in London but his career was made in Adelaide, South Australia. He married Mary Ann Collins before leaving for Australia and all their children were born in Adelaide.

Julia was born in the murky conditions of Whitechapel and would die a wealthy woman in an altogether more desirable part of London. Before she, too, went to Australia she married David Cohen, brother-in-law of her sister, Rachel.

Miriam, like the rest of her family, started her life in east London before travelling to Australia. She married Benjamin Solomon in 1841 and the couple made their fortune in Australia, in between a vigorous period of procreating which resulted in twelve children. When they returned to England, she could afford a staff of nine servants, including a coachman and a page.

Esther was only thirteen when she emigrated in the company of her brother, David. Three years later she married Moses Moss (who was the brother of Birdie Moss's grandfather). Unlike most of her family she stayed in Australia, where she died in 1893.

The Children of Moses

The course of life for the family of Moses and Rosetta Joseph followed a different path from that of the Nathans, as the couple were required by law to remain in Australia for the foreseeable future. All of their eleven children were, therefore, born there so the decision of whether to emigrate did not apply.

Moss
The Tribe of Moses

The Josephs' eleven children were all born over a twenty-year period between 1833 and 1853. Not all of them remained permanently in Australia and some moved to and from England more than once in the course of their lifetime. Those who finally settled in England all did so in fashionable parts of London, each a world apart from the East End that was the original home of their parents. They all fared well. Hyam Joseph, for instance, owned a large cattle station and became first mayor of Bombala, NSW.

Other than Hyam, in order of age, there were Caroline, Charlotte, Sarah, Lewis, Arthur, Miriam, Alice, David, Joseph and Julia. These are all just names, of course, but also real people I am descended from on my maternal grandmother's side.

(...cont'd)

The records give names and dates, as well as places and occupations, but were they to be alive today there are so many questions I would like to ask. If Australia could offer so much, why did so many of you eventually return to England? When you came back, did you visit areas like Whitechapel and Spitalfields, where it all started? Would you have valued the sense of community in those districts and would that have outweighed their material deprivation? In contrast, what was it about Australia that was most important to you? Did you talk to your father about his own experience – of how he was punished and then made a success of his life? And your mother, too – whether she had any doubts before travelling on her own to the new colony and the trust she put in her husband-to-be. With eleven children to bring up, was she able as well to take an active interest in her husband's business ventures?

So many questions, so much unknown. Just a few generations back but now out of reach. One can only seek the most tenuous of footholds to get a glimpse of what it was like. But the underlying emotions, the joy and sorrow of experience – that is lost forever.

Hyam Moses Joseph (seated centre of middle row) at Maharatta Station, Bombala, NSW

Australasia was the magnet that drew these early relatives, and it became the focus of their lives. But, as we will see in the following sections, there were other parts of the world which also feature for different family members. Some ventured to the Americas and to southern Africa, lured by thoughts of freedom, new business opportunities and, perhaps, that lingering sense of wanderlust engendered by many previous years in the diaspora.

Atlantic Crossings

Land of the West, we come to thee,
Far over the desert of the sea.[38]

It was probably inevitable that many Jews migrated to the Americas – to the Latin territories in the south, to the colonies that became the United States, and to the French and British possessions that later formed Canada. Such were the westward routes taken by numerous ships crowded with migrants from all parts of Europe, a rich combination of cultures and religions, Jews and non-Jews alike. If there was a common motive that bound them together it was the incentive to leave Europe and find a home in lands that were renowned for their freedom. Opportunities abounded and the vessels that crossed the Atlantic were, for successive generations, full of hopeful souls in search of new lives.

For the Jews, who were part of this westward flow, whether they headed to the north or south of the Americas depended initially on their different backgrounds. One might have thought that Latin America held a greater attraction for Sephardi Jews with their own Spanish and Portuguese origins. In fact they were no more welcome there, if they were not Catholics, than in the Iberian countries they had been forced to leave and many went, instead, to colonies in the region controlled by the more tolerant Dutch or British. Gradually, however, the pattern changed and today the most numerous of the 600,000 Jews who settled on this continent live in Argentina, which contains about half of all who found new homes in Latin America, followed by Brazil.

Abdela

Moving Continents

There is some evidence that a few of my own relatives made their home in Argentina and possibly Brazil too.[39] Certainly, Joseph Shasha (originally from Baghdad) and his wife, Rachel (daughter of Jacob Elia Abdela) were amongst these. The couple had married in Manchester in 1909 and in the 1930s were living comfortably, close to other Sephardi families in the Withington district. Joseph was by then well established in the city and (in partnership with his nephew, Khedouri) was making a success of a shipping company that specialized in trade with the Middle East. Yet, in spite of the comfort of their lives, Joseph and Rachel decided it was time to move. Joseph (who was then a foreign national) had been interned as 'an alien enemy' in 1914. It had been a painful experience and, if another war broke out, he feared he might still be regarded as such.[40] That would not have been the case as by then he had British citizenship, but the memory of his previous encounter with the authorities, together with the virulent anti-Semitism that could be seen in Germany, made it all seem too close for comfort.

Joseph and Rachel's daughter, Marjorie, had already moved to New York, but they chose, instead, to relocate with their family to Buenos Aires. Business was booming in that part of the world and Joseph soon established himself in imports and exports, mainly in the textile trade that he knew so well. Harrods, the London emporium, had its only overseas foreign store in the Argentinian capital, and his company was a regular supplier.

After the war, Joseph and Rachel moved back to Manchester, but one of their sons, Eric, stayed on in Argentina. He took over the business and remained in Buenos Aires until his death in 1981.

Another early destination for Jews on the move was Canada. The first Jewish settlers congregated, especially, in the city of Montreal, although numbers in those early days were not large.[41] Members of the Moss family were amongst the first arrivals, including David, an uncle of my maternal grandmother. The Mosses made their way from the East End of London, although before that there are links to Alsace and Holland. When they arrived in the northern colony, in the early to mid-nineteenth century, there was only one synagogue, Spanish and Portuguese, but new ones were built for the increasing number of Ashkenazim coming to the country. In fact, David Moss (formerly Moses) was active in helping to start one of the latter in Montreal, where he is credited with laying the foundation stone.[42] Like some of the other pioneering families, the Mosses decided not to remain in Canada, returning to England in around 1880. In some ways, it was a strange decision and against the general trend. As they looked from the decks on their eastward-bound voyage they might well have seen ships travelling in the opposite direction, taking a new wave of migrants from the increasingly-troubled countries of central and eastern Europe. The attraction of Canada continued in the period before and after the Second World War, and, over the years, the Jewish population there has grown to a present total of some 400,000.

In terms of numbers, though, it was the United States which was by far the most important destination, with peaks of migration occurring in the last quarter of the nineteenth century and early decades of the next, followed by the decision of Jews in large numbers to leave Europe during and after the domination of the Nazis in Germany. There were attempts by the US Government to curb the original influx but these did not prevent a steady build-up to reach the present total in the country, now in the region of 5.7 million. The population in both the US and Israel accounts for about 80% of the world's Jewry. Although small in relation to the total American population, the Jewish minority exercises an important influence on the nation's foreign policy, which has remined steadfastly supportive of the Zionist cause.

Abdela

New York, New York

In spite of the general popularity of America amongst Jews fleeing from Europe, relatively few of my own family joined the exodus.[43] Having reached England, most were content to find a niche in the likes of London or Manchester, where they stayed.

There were, of course, individuals who decided to venture further, and, in Chapter 4, I tell the story of one relative who was drawn by the glamour of Hollywood. But there were few instances of whole families moving to America. One exception (mentioned above) was the Shasha family, whose connection with the Abdelas came when Joseph Shasha married Rachel, one of the daughters of Jacob Elia Abdela.

When they met, Joseph and Rachel were both living in Manchester, where Joseph had built up his shipping business. Although the couple remained in England, it seems that their only daughter, Marjorie, moved to New York and married there. With her husband, they started a family which led to a new lineage, spreading through the generations to other parts of the country.

The other example, Angelo Salomon Abdela, was more directly related, as his great-grandfather was a brother of Jacob Elia Abdela. Angelo was born in Egypt in 1942 and applied for US naturalization in 1985. At the time of writing, he still lives in New York, and associates himself with international strategy and finance.

Out of Africa

I have no special corner in my heart for the ghetto: I am at home in the entire world, where there are clouds and birds and human tears.[44]

The above words, spoken by the Zionist pioneer and leading campaigner, Rosa Luxemburg, have a special resonance for Jews in the diaspora constantly searching for new ways to leave the ghetto. And where better than Africa to discover a world 'where there are clouds and birds and human tears'?

When they first left their homeland in the eastern Mediterranean, many turned west and followed the northern shores of the African continent. From Egypt along the coast, ultimately to Morocco, groups gathered and communities were formed, generally living peacefully with their new neighbours. Their numbers were later augmented after fellow Jews were expelled from Spain and Portugal. In fact, the Jewish presence in essentially Arab countries worked well and lasted without serious interruption for centuries. Only with the establishment of Israel in 1948 were they no longer welcome and, fearing outright hostility, many recognized it was time to leave. Currently, there are few, if any, Jews left along this stretch of the Mediterranean coastline.

Meanwhile, most of sub-Saharan Africa never had the same attraction as a place to settle. In spite of its valuable resources and the potential to trade, it was a difficult environment and not conducive to large-scale immigration. Only in the south of the continent – where the climate was more amenable and where there was a rich source of gold and diamonds – did Jews in large numbers choose to make their home. From as early as the seventeenth century, they settled in what became South Africa, where they took a leading role in mining and exports. But their presence was initially small, and it was not until the last quarter of the nineteenth century before others (overwhelmingly from Europe and Russia) arrived in large numbers. Most settled in Johannesburg and Cape Town but some also explored the neighbouring colonies to the north, including Southern Rhodesia, which saw the emergence of small but thriving Jewish communities in Bulawayo and Salisbury.

By the time of the First World War, the Jewish community in South Africa numbered at least 40,000, a figure which rose to a peak of close to 120,000 in the 1970s.[45] Since then, there has been an outward flow, to Israel and other destinations like Canada and Australia, and the total has fallen to little more than 50,000. Likewise, Zimbabwe (formerly Southern Rhodesia) has seen the decline of its previously active Jewish community to a total of barely one hundred. The main reason for this sizeable emigration from both South Africa and Zimbabwe is not the traditional one of anti-Semitism so much as the everyday difficulties of living in the region.

My own relatives were not heavily involved in this particular aspect of the diaspora, but nor were they absent. It only takes one member of a family to open a new vista and, in this way, Joseph Abdela (one of the sons of

Jacob Elia), was one such pathfinder. For him and his successors, southern Africa provided the lure and for the Abdelas it became a new place to add to their varied provenance, a further strand in the family tree.

Abdela

Paradise Lost

Joseph Abdela was one of six brothers, the sons of Jacob Elia Abdela, who all grew up in and around Manchester. He appears in photos, often with an impish smile, sporting a full, brush moustache, and invariably wearing a dark suit and white shirt with a winged collar. His appearance suggests the confident young businessman that he was. Very presentable in appearance, he was in his mid-twenties when he married Sarah Dorothy Lazarus. In due course, the couple had two children, Hannah Muriel (who became Wooley through marriage) and Jacob Samuel (who was to become a High Court judge).

Business was good until the end of the First World War, after which Joseph could sense the first chill winds of change. Competition with other countries was keener and Manchester, with its ageing infrastructure, was no longer so dominant in world markets. By the mid-1920s, the situation had become serious and Joseph feared that he would be unable to keep his family in the way he wished. As his grand-daughter light-heartedly recalls from a tale told by her mother, he was ashamed to reveal that he ate his own jam sandwiches for lunch in his office. But Joseph was resourceful and unwilling to preside over decline. It was time, he believed, to leave Manchester and find fresh opportunities in the New World. For him, southern Africa (not only South Africa but also neighbouring colonies), rich in resources and with trade still in its infancy, was the place to be. The decision was taken, and on 13 August 1926, ahead of his wife and children, he set sail from Southampton aboard the 'SS Balmoral Castle', bound for Port Elizabeth in South Africa.

From Port Elizabeth the overland trip northwards to his chosen destination, Bulawayo, in Southern Rhodesia, must have been an adventure in itself. But, for all the change – a world away from Manchester – it seems that he adapted well to his new environment.

One can only speculate why he chose to settle in Bulawayo but the fact that there was at that time a thriving Jewish community would have helped him with useful contacts and advice.

Joseph's granddaughter, Barbara Wicks, picks up the story of what it was like in Bulawayo, recalling a happy childhood in a land of sunshine:

> *In Bulawayo the family became very well-respected and the company of J.J. Abdela was formed and became one of the premier wholesalers in Southern Rhodesia and beyond. The range of goods was quite extreme, from foodstuffs to imported toys...*
>
> *The house in Bulawayo where my grandparents lived was freestanding on a large plot of land. The wider community in Kumalo (a neighbourhood in Bulawayo) was predominantly Jewish and there was a beautiful synagogue in the centre of the city. While my grandpa devoted a lot of time to building his new business, my grandma was able to concentrate on her music. She was a very talented artist in her own right and as a musician unsurpassed. Her contralto voice was superb and she sang in many local performances. Music must have run in the family as my mother later taught music and dancing to anyone in the community who wished to learn.*
>
> *I had the most blissful and happy childhood and friends made in my youth are still friends today. We had the freedom of riding bikes to the dam and fishing for tilapia, which we cooked on a fire at the water's edge. Or we gathered at the municipal pool in town and a million other great meeting places. When I reached the dreaded age of eleven, I was packed off to boarding school in Salisbury and only had the company of my wonderful friends during school holidays. Those were the best days of all, riding the horses and going in the buggy (more like a cart) to see a film at the drive-in cinema down the road.*
>
> *I lived with my parents on a smallholding, in a magnificent house carved from the granite that was all around. It was called MKulu Moya (meaning 'great winds') because of the strong gusts that blew across the open landscape, interrupted only by the granite outcrops known as 'koppies'. In the distance were seductive views of a mountain range. All of that was my home. Rhodesia then was a blooming paradise, nurtured and loved, and still is by so many; unfortunately, neglect and mismanagement has crippled the economy and the country has degenerated into a desert.*

(...cont'd)

When my grandma died, my mother helped her father with the business and when he, too, passed away both of my parents stepped in to keep it running. I went on to attend university in South Africa, which is when I met and married my husband. At first, we settled in Johannesburg, before moving with our two daughters to Natal, which is where I still live. Sadly, my husband passed away in 1985.

Chapter 4

Business Matters

There is a common assumption that Jews are good at business. People point to successful Jewish leaders in the world of business and commerce to support their claim. As we will see in the rest of this chapter, there are many instances of my own family members who were, indeed, remarkably successful in this way. But was that because of circumstances or a result of some kind of genetic programming? Did success come naturally or was it a question of necessity?

I have not come across any scientific evidence to show that genes are the cause. And, apart from anything else, if genes were to offer a golden key then why are so many Jews (myself very much included) an exception to the rule. The popular link, I suspect, is not unrelated to anti-Semitism, rooted in a lingering image of Jews in the counting house. Far more convincing, and palatable, is the idea that in the long struggle against persecution business offered one of the few ways in which outsiders could secure a foothold in society. Motivation was not only a question of material security but also a way of gaining acceptance amongst an established elite. If one doubts this, there is the compelling story of the Rothschild family in England to illustrate the argument.[46]

The family in question came, originally, from the German city of Frankfurt. During the fifteenth century they lived out of the limelight, like other Jews at the time, in a designated ghetto. In spite of these inauspicious beginnings, plans were subsequently laid for the family to enter the world of banking. While Frankfurt provided a starting-point for their activities, during the nineteenth century they established themselves in other European cities too, including London.

The family worked together, with different members heading the various country projects. And they shared a belief that their dealings should always be beyond reproach, gaining a reputation not only for the probity of their transactions but also for their respect for government protocols. What is more, their accumulation of great wealth was matched by acts of well-regarded, and also well-publicized, philanthropy.

Circumstances favoured their arrival on the English banking scene in the early nineteenth century. For one thing, their skilful handling of the business of raising capital and dispensing payments during the Napoleonic wars was readily acknowledged. From that they went on to underwrite large-scale investments in infrastructure and other activities across the British Empire. On both counts, they made progress in the first half of the century, in spite of numerous restrictions on what Jews were allowed to do (a situation that applied across Europe and not just in England). But the Rothschilds saw the way the tide was running in their favour and were prepared to wait, quietly, through their example making the case for greater acceptance rather than actively lobbying for change. At no point did they seek the easy option of religious conversion in order to make their operations easier. In time, emancipation was extended so that Jews could at last undertake business and lead their lives on the same basis as anyone else.

Place is important in England in signalling social status, and the Rothschilds were adept at finding very high-quality properties. In London, these were centred around a cluster of historic buildings where the prestigious Park Lane meets Piccadilly, the very hub of fashionable society; just across Hyde Park Corner was the outer wall of Buckingham Palace. At the same time, in the countryside they bought extensive estates where they could entertain on a par with some of the most established landed gentry. They were careful in how they handled political and social relations, extending their network of influence without arousing needless opposition. Benjamin Disraeli was an obvious friend but so, too, was his political opponent, William Gladstone. The Rothschilds were also admitted into royal circles and mixed with some of the most respected families of the aristocracy.

Although this banking dynasty was hardly representative of the wider Jewish community, where individuals sought in more modest ways to secure their own place in the world of business, the example of the Rothschilds was undoubtedly inspirational. Who knows to what extent some of my own ancestors would have thought, 'well, if the Rothschilds can break through the barriers, so can I'? In fact, if they did have those thoughts, most of them started from a greatly inferior position, as the poorest of immigrants in the East End. But they were not to be deterred.

'Rags to Riches'

Dear God, you made many, many poor people.
I realize, of course, that it's no shame to be poor
But it's no great honor, either.
So what would have been so terrible if I had a small fortune?[47]

It is a cliché to describe a business success story as one of 'rags to riches'. Business success rarely starts with rags, while riches can only be relative. Yet there is a sense in some past stories that this simple imagery is just what it was. No-one, for instance, can read Israel Zangwill's perceptive account of penniless refugees arriving in the East End in the last quarter of the nineteenth century without agreeing that the starting point was, indeed, one of rags.

Any prospect of riches to come was surely illusory. Yet, given time, the transition happens. To take just one of his colourful characters, Baruch Emanuel is first portrayed as a penniless cobbler, working all hours, driven only by his obsession to outdo his arch-rival, Mordecai Schwartz. He puts notices on his grimy window, advertising for assistants that he cannot afford but wanting to appear more successful than he really was. But Zangwill observed that people in that position will, over time, improve their lot. That is why, when he returns to see how Baruch was faring, he finds that things have become very different. By then:

> He had several establishments and owned five two-storey houses, and
> was treasurer of his little synagogue, and spoke of Socialists as an inferior
> variety of Atheists. Not that all this bourgeoning was to be counted to
> leather, for Baruch had developed enterprises in all directions.[48]

Although no doubt drawn from a degree of reality, Baruch Emanuel was a fictional character – a poor man who was well on his way to making good. Some of my own relatives, however, could illustrate even better this trajectory from the humblest of beginnings to enormous success in business. The two families from which the best examples are drawn have already been introduced in the previous chapter, the Nathans and the Josephs. It is time now to show the various paths they took to make their fortunes; and it is hard to describe this as anything other than a series of transformations from rags to riches.

Nathan's Formula

Like many individuals who make a success of business, the basic formula is quite simple. Nathan Nathan, as we have seen, was given his introduction to Australia around the turn of the eighteenth and nineteenth centuries, when the colony was largely what the Europeans saw as virgin territory. After seven years he returned to England but in that short time he had seen enough to know what was possible. And he inspired every one of his children to follow in his footsteps.

There was nothing complicated about what needed to be done. For a start, bringing across essential goods like tools and farm implements, as well as consumables like clothing and fabrics, could hardly fail to yield a profit. The new colonists would be unable to make progress without these. And once sufficient capital was accumulated, every opportunity could be taken to buy property, whether a basic shop or a stretch of forest. The value of these early acquisitions would surely appreciate as the land was settled, and with it the wealth of the far-sighted investors. But there was also a third variable in the formula and that was hard work. In order to succeed, no effort could be spared and competition should always be outpaced.

And, basically, the Nathan family did just that, taking sometimes small steps to start with but always moving in the same direction, from rags to riches. Below we can see some of the activities which made them a very prosperous family.

Moss

Colonial Capitalists

One of the sons, Louis Nathan, for instance, decided that Tasmania offered promise and so he settled in the capital, Hobart, where he opened a store. Always on the lookout for new opportunities, it was not long before he also invested in shipping, both whalers and trading vessels. When he later returned with his wife to London they are to be found in fashionable addresses, first in Finsbury Circus on the northern edge of the City, then York Terrace (close to Regent's Park). They had no children but at both addresses the couple were served by domestic staff comprising a lady's maid, footman, cook and housemaid. It appears he may also have owned another property, in Tavistock Square. Louis died, in 1866 at the age of fifty-three, leaving in his will a sum of more than £75,000 (equivalent to about £9 million today) to members of his family.

Other Nathans also left very large sums in their wills and lived in some of the most favoured parts of London. Julia married a merchant, David Cohen, and when they, too, returned from Australia they occupied houses, first, in Tavistock Square and then Lancaster Gate. David died in 1901, leaving what was then the colossal sum of more than £200,000.

Miriam and Solomon Benjamin, meanwhile, lived with their twelve children in Harlow House, Brunswick Place, with a staff of nine servants including a coachman and a page. Business was obviously good and no doubt there was more than a little one-upmanship between different family members. How could you possibly manage without a coachman, one might ask?

There is no evidence that anyone actually failed but, inevitably, some fared better than others, David Nathan being a case in point. David built his businesses in New Zealand. He is recorded as a merchant, auctioneer, shipping agent and community leader but even that does not fully describe his many activities, which included owning several small trading vessels and extensive property holdings in Auckland. He is best known, though, for his legacy brand, L.D. Nathan & Co., a consolidated company that remains a major player in the Australasian food and drink industry and is the subject of a publication *As Old as Auckland*.[49]

Moses and the Golden Touch

The family of Moses Joseph was no less successful, following a path that embraced a wide range of activities and which also led to considerable wealth – another colourful illustration of rags to riches.

Moss

Casting off the Shackles

Five years after Moses had stepped off the convict ship, 'Albion', his fiancée, Rosetta, arrived in Sydney. Moses had by then been given a job with a firm of Jewish merchants and so, with a record of good standing since he arrived, the couple wasted no time in petitioning the Governor to be married. This was duly sanctioned and the wedding took place in 1832, marking one of the first traditional Jewish marriages in Australasia. Moreover, Moses was granted a certificate of exemption, which meant that he could be employed by his new wife. They opened a tobacco shop, which did well, and in 1839 Moses was granted a conditional pardon. From that point on there was no stopping the couple, neither commercially nor in producing numerous offspring. New South Wales was, indeed, fertile ground for the aspiring.

First, they invested in a weatherboard property in the centre of Sydney, which they soon replaced with a three-storey building called Commercial House. Moving into an altogether higher league, they then acquired the leasehold of 50,000 acres of land in the south of the colony, before venturing into the business of trading in wool. The arrival of his brother, Israel, as a free settler encouraged a further venture, this time into the packing of canned meat and other produce, gaining them the reputation of being the first food processors in the colony. With success in business assured, it then helped that in 1848 the award of an absolute pardon released him from the last fetters of the past; he no longer carried the tag of a convict.

Even without the full pardon, he had been uninhibited in growing his business and was always looking to cross new frontiers. Now, like other Jewish settlers in the colony, he saw business opportunities in owning ships and engaging in trade, not only along the lengthy coastline of his home shores but also across the stormy sea that separated Australia from New Zealand.

With a fleet of fourteen ships to his name, it gave him special pride in 1847 to name the latest one after his wife, 'Rosetta Joseph'. When he heard about the California Gold Rush of 1848, he was quick to arrange for his prized ship to be loaded with merchandise that would be in demand in the goldfields. Although it was gold which lured prospectors in their thousands, there was money to be made from more mundane items like shovels and buckets, wheel-barrows and hand tools.

A successful crossing across the Pacific was made but on the return voyage the 'Rosetta Joseph' foundered on rocks, still 700 kilometres from the Australian mainland. At least the sad story has a silver lining, as all on board were saved and the craft itself was adequately insured. Undeterred by the incident at sea, and although he was making profits from sundry items, Moses kept his sights firmly on the value of gold itself. His interest was boosted by the fact that there was a coincident gold rush in Australia, not only in the colony where he lived but also in neighbouring Victoria. By 1852 he had become the largest licensed gold buyer and exporter in New South Wales. Moses was by then a very wealthy man and felt free to devote more of his time to giving something back to the community.

The Glaxo Story

The success achieved by both Nathan Nathan and Moses Joseph, and their respective offspring, was matched by that of another relation, Joseph Nathan. Not merely matched but in some ways surpassed, as Joseph set in train a sequence of events which led to the formation of what eventually became the multinational corporation, Glaxo (which, in turn evolved into the pharmaceutical giant, GlaxoSmithKline). Business ingenuity clearly ran in the family, although the humble start of a general store in New Zealand in the pioneering days of Auckland was hardly a clue for what was to come. Like his uncles, Joseph fathered a large family and his seven sons were variously involved in the expanding business.

While Joseph was still chairing the company, their breakthrough came when they saw an opportunity to produce baby food by drying milk, the secret of their success being the addition of sugar as an essential part of the process. The original name chosen was Lacto, but this was changed to Glaxo when it was found that other firms were already trading under the former name.

Moss

The Nathan's... Again[50]

Joseph Edward Nathan was born in 1835 in Christ Church Spitalfields in the same part of east London as other members of the Nathan and Joseph families. He was the sixth son and eighth child of Rachel Davis and her husband, Edward Ezekiel Nathan, a tailor (the latter being a cousin of Moses Joseph).

Like other members of his family who went on to make a fortune in one of the new colonies, he started life with few material advantages and received very little formal education. At the age of twelve, Joseph started work alongside his father as a jobbing tailor. Later he got a job in a furniture store and at the same time attended evening classes at Bishopsgate Institute.

In August 1853, at the age of eighteen, he emigrated to Australia, arriving four months later in Melbourne on the 'William Ackers'. There he opened a miners' supply store behind a hotel in Little Collins Street. Because his prospects in Melbourne were limited by lack of capital, Nathan looked for new opportunities in New Zealand, where several of his relatives had already settled.

His sister, Kate, had married a Wellington merchant, Jacob Joseph (another relative of the Nathans) who, although handicapped by blindness, had prospered. Late in 1856 Joseph Nathan visited Wellington where Jacob Joseph, who was planning a trip to England, offered him employment. Nathan accepted the offer on condition that he would receive a salary of £300 per annum plus a share of profits. For a man of twenty-one, he struck a hard bargain.

Before starting his new job, he returned to Melbourne, wound up his affairs there, and on 18 November 1857 married Dinah Marks in a Jewish ceremony. The newlyweds arrived back in Wellington on the 'Cheetah' on 9 December 1857. They were to have at least thirteen children, of whom eleven – seven boys and four girls – were to survive to adulthood.

Jacob Joseph and Company imported goods from England to supply the retail trade. Soap, candles, tar, ironware, stationery, drapery, groceries and patent medicines were unloaded in the company's Wellington warehouse, and orders were dispatched to the various stores by horse-drawn wagons or bullock carts. In time, the company also bought wool from local farmers for export, and in season sold butter in Wellington's markets.

Jacob Joseph's Residence and Store, Lambton Quay

On 1 January 1861, Nathan was made a partner of Jacob Joseph and Company. The Nathan family then lived in the company's storehouse on Lambton Quay. Business hours conformed to Jewish practice, with the sabbath observed without fail. Nathan became a leader of the Wellington Hebrew Congregation; he was President from 1870 to 1874 and initiated the building of a synagogue, consecrated in 1870.

Always looking for new opportunities, Joseph Nathan bought land in the interior and by 1867 held one of the largest areas in Manawatu. One purchase method – viewed by some as sharp practice – involved buying land certificates (issued by the government in lieu of payment) from soldiers returning from active service. These government land grants, for which Nathan generally paid £25, were of moderate size but variable quality.

Nathan's senior partner, Jacob Joseph, was a much older man and known to be difficult to work with; the partnership was duly dissolved on 26 June 1873. After Jacob Joseph retired, Nathan purchased the assets of the business and consolidated his activities into Joseph Nathan and Company. He built a new four-storeyed office building on the corner of Grey and Featherstone Streets and a substantial family home in Hawkestone Street.

(...cont'd)

In 1876 Nathan established a London office and secured funds for capital expansion. Back in New Zealand, assisted by his eldest son, David, he rebuilt his business, which had suffered from his lack of attention while he was abroad and was on the verge of bankruptcy. David did much of the travelling, by coastal vessel and on horseback with saddle-bags full of samples. By the end of the 1870s, Nathan had acquired an interest in a number of retail outlets including a Ready Money Store in Palmerston North, which later became the Manawatu Farmers' Co-operative Association Store.

Perhaps mindful of anti-Semitic attitudes in colonial society, Joseph Nathan kept a careful distance from politics. In business he strove to diversify family interests and to get involved in a wide range of trade and commercial activities in Wellington. In 1870 he was a founding director of the Wellington Patent Slip Company and in 1876 a founding committee member of the Wellington and Wairarapa Grand Trunk Tramway Company. He became a director of the Wellington Gas Company, the New Zealand Candle Company and the Wellington Woollen Manufacturing Company and was President of the Wellington Chamber of Commerce in 1881. He helped set up the Wellington Harbour Board and, with others, inaugurated the Wellington and Manawatu Railway Company in 1881. As its chairman of directors, Nathan officiated at the 'last spike' railway completion ceremony on 3 November 1886.

From 1887 onwards, the senior Nathans lived in England. Joseph's wife Dinah died at sea, between Portugal and Madeira, in 1893. Afterwards, Joseph visited New Zealand several times but resigned his directorships in favour of his eldest son. Joseph Nathan and Company was registered as a limited company in London on 19 July 1899 with a capital value of £127,000. While Joseph Nathan was chairman and retained control of finances, all of his sons were in some way involved in company business: Louis, Maurice and later Alexander in England; David, Philip, Frederick and, later, Charles in New Zealand.

But the real *coup de grâce* was still to come. From 1901 to 1903 the Nathans negotiated for the rights to manufacture dried milk in New Zealand. They employed an engineer to install milk-drying machinery in the Nathans' Makino dairy factory near Feilding. In 1904 they built a new dried-milk factory at Bunnythorpe, designed specifically for new production methods. Although twice sabotaged in its first year, from 1906 the factory manufactured dried milk in addition to cheese and other dairy products. Alexander Nathan went to England in 1907 and organized the marketing of dried milk (which was registered as Glaxo in October 1906), using the once-famous slogan 'Builds Bonnie Babies'. In 1937 control of dairy product manufacture was transferred to Glaxo, by then a separate company and on its way to becoming a multinational corporation.

Joseph Nathan died in London on 2 May 1912. Although the company was based in London, a Wellington office continued to supply imported merchandise to all parts of New Zealand, while a dairying branch manufactured and exported dried milk, butter and cheese to other countries. By his energy and business foresight, Joseph Nathan played a major part in developing New Zealand's export dairy industry.

'Men of Substance'

Commerce is a noble profession, and Jews should get over any self-hatred they might harbor from contemplating the capitalist spirit of diaspora Judaism.[51]

It would be disingenuous to exaggerate the sense of a rift between the two main groupings of Judaism, the Sephardi and Ashkenazi. Certainly, there are differences between the two. But, given the separate paths they took in the diaspora, that in itself is hardly surprising. Inevitably, they absorbed varying aspects of language and culture in their adopted homelands, and over time religious practice itself took its own course. In spite of these differences, however, both groups remained steadfastly Jewish and to the outside world there would have been little evidence of a division. Yet one cannot ignore informal attitudes which create needless barriers between the two.

In short, there has for long been a suggestion that Sephardi Jews are somehow superior: that 'Sephardim saw themselves as Jewish nobility'.[52] This view is based on the fact that theirs was primarily a Mediterranean and Middle Eastern culture, closely aligned to the parallel development of an Arab civilization. As such, they played an active role in the countries where they were accepted, gaining respect for their artistic contributions and also renowned as physicians and scholars. They were even trusted sufficiently to serve in government posts and in the royal courts, and to represent their country as diplomats. And, invariably, they were successful in business and trade, traditional areas of strength in Jewish communities. Some of my own relatives, for instance, engaged in aspects of Mediterranean shipping and formed an influential body of merchants.

In contrast, the Ashkenazim often lacked the same opportunities to serve their respective nations, rarely being trusted and invariably regarded as aliens. Certain professions were denied to them and they were often dispersed across the countryside, a result of being forced by statute to live outside the towns and cities. Both the Sephardim and Ashkenazim suffered persecution but for the latter it continued, in central and eastern Europe, in brutal form through to the twentieth century. When they fled the nineteenth-century pogroms, they arrived penniless and often without a profession in the countries that would accept them. This stood in contrast with the better standing of their Sephardi brothers and sisters. It was perhaps inevitable, though unfortunate, that their relative deprivation would be compared with the more fortunate circumstances of the Sephardim. In time, of course, the differences inherited by the two diminished and, to the outside world, they were simply Jewish.

The contrast when they arrived in England is well summarized in the following extract by an observer at the time:

> The original immigrants into England from Germany and Poland were undoubtedly placed at a great disadvantage as regards the Spanish and Portuguese settlers. These latter were usually men of wealth, of polished manners, of old lineage, whose ancestors had constantly figured at courts, and who in modern times had constituted an aristocracy of commerce in Holland. The former were persons whose forefathers for ages had been subjected to every kind of degrading persecution, and had been debarred from pursuing any ennobling avocations; persons who themselves had neither been endowed by their fathers with worldly goods nor with liberal knowledge.[53]

My own family contains elements of both traditions. There are the Ashkenazim who were strongly (but not solely) rooted in the East End of London, and the Sephardim who were drawn to the opportunities provided by the cotton industry centred on Manchester. In the latter, they arrived with money from their previous mercantile activities in Arta and Corfu, and they went on to establish themselves as successful families in their new country. Ironically, as we have seen, the Nathan and Joseph families, East End Ashkenazim through and through, with no money or trades to get started, turned everything on its head and emerged as the wealthiest of all my relatives.

From Father to Son

Jacob Elia Abdela was already a man of substance when he took the decision to leave Corfu with his family and start a new life in Manchester. There were good economic reasons for doing so but also, no doubt, he knew that a secure life in Corfu depended on the precarious nature of international relations in the region. It was a brave decision to give up what he already had but it transpired that it was also the right one. Like other Sephardi families who came to Manchester, in due course they could all expect to lead comfortable lives. They had no trouble in creating opportunities in business, they were at home in the emergent Jewish community, and they would live in the kind of grand house with servants that was expected of them. The story of Isaac, one of Jacob Elia's six sons, is illustrative of how they fared.

Abdela

Isaac's Boats

An important chapter in the history of my family is the contribution made by my grandfather, Isaac Abdela. Young Isaac arrived in Manchester with his parents and his two older brothers in 1875. As he grew up, his father would have told him about his own background as a shipping merchant in the Mediterranean and the fascination he found in helping trade to flourish across the sea he knew so well. From an early age, Isaac was attracted to the idea, and, to prepare himself, he trained as an engineer, duly attending the Technical School in Manchester and then learning his trade through working with reputable firms in the region. In one of these firms, he was nominated for Associate Membership of the Institute of Naval Architects.

While still in his twenties, Isaac had already established himself in business in Manchester. At one address he is recorded as a manufacturer of a small type of river launch called a slipper, as well as offering services in glass-cutting and general engineering.

(...cont'd)

"DUX", believed to have been built for a tug firm at Bristol. Mr. Abdela standing by the boiler.

Meanwhile, at a different venue, his activities were registered as 'Shippers and Agents'. With an eye to the future, he saw an opportunity to rent the premises of an ailing company at Brimscombe in Gloucestershire, on the then busy Thames and Severn Canal. It included two manufacturing areas, Hope Mill Yard and Canal Ironworks, with facilities for boatbuilding. Within eighteen months the original company folded and Isaac was in a prime position to acquire the whole firm at auction. As part of his grand strategy, in 1901 (when still only twenty-seven) he merged his present company in Manchester with grey cloth merchants, Mitchell and Company. Following this, the company of Abdela and Mitchell was formed, heralding the start of a new venture in shipbuilding.[54]

For the best part of a quarter of a century, Abdela and Mitchell gained a dual reputation, first as a local employer in Brimscombe but also internationally for its well-constructed river and harbour boats. Many of them were designed on similar lines, suitable for plying the major rivers of Africa and South America. To give an idea of the typical design, when the iconic film, 'The African Queen', starring Humphrey Bogart and Katherine Hepburn, was released in 1951, it was quite widely suggested that the boat itself was a product of the Abdela and Mitchell boatyard. Although others have given technical reasons to show that this was unlikely, there is more than a hint of romance that runs through the history of the works. One of the early orders, for instance, was for a steamer, named the 'Adis Ababa' *(sic)* and four prefabricated steel punts to support an expedition to the Blue Nile.

"CAROLINA" built for South America. Mr. Abdela standing nearest the stern.

Similar orders followed, one being for no fewer than seventeen river boats for use on the Amazon. The industrial archaeologist, A.M. Langford makes an interesting connection when he suggests that the reason why so many of their orders originated in South America might be because members of the Abdela family 'had migrated from Corfu to Egypt, and some had later gone thence to Brazil...'[55] In other words, there might well have been established family links and opportunities to serve interests on both sides of the Atlantic.

Another romantic association followed the marriage in 1903 of Isaac to Birdie Moss. Where better for a honeymoon than a trip to the Mediterranean, where his ancestors had for so long lived? He chose an alluring itinerary that included the French Riviera, Italy and Greece, an itinerary that could hardly have failed to impress his new wife. But was there also a business motive in doing this as, in that same year, his company was ready to deliver a new craft, the 'Haroony', from the Brimscombe yard to a destination in Turkey? If it were to sail under its own steam, one can see the temptation to provide free passage for the illustrious voyage.

Naming some of his boats after his children was another way in which Isaac would mix business with pleasure. His elder daughter, Iris, inspired the name of a 53-foot vessel, while a design was prepared for the 'Violet', presumably named after his younger daughter (my mother), although there is no evidence that this was completed. Family connections were important and it was probably no surprise that other Abdelas were to join the flourishing business. One of Isaac's brothers, Joseph, became a director in 1912 and from that point he may well have held the majority of shares in the company. There is also evidence of another brother, Elia, relocating to be close to the boatyard (living at Brimscombe Court) and no doubt he too had in interest in the business. One of Elia's two daughters was Mary, who, although born in Constantinople, was to live in Stroud (close to Brimscombe) for most of her life. Her appearance spoke of the eastern Mediterranean, but in her ways she was as English as the Gloucestershire country town where she lived and worked.

On the strength of the success of the business, and with the probable source of additional investment from Joseph, it was time to expand. Consequently, the search was on for another working site, culminating in the acquisition of the Dee Shipbuilding Yard at Queensferry in north-east Wales. The site was not far from Manchester, with its many business connections already known to the Abdelas, and it enjoyed access from the mouth of the River Dee to the open sea. Two of the early products built under new ownership were tugs for the Port of Marseilles. One of the advantages of the Queensferry works was that it was possible to produce larger craft, such as the 150-foot river steamer, 'Lobao'. In the years leading up to the First World War, orders held up quite well at Queensbury but at Brimscombe the collapse of the Amazon rubber trade ended production of additional river boats for that region. Wartime orders offered some relief but business in the postwar period diminished at both centres.

An uninsured fire which destroyed the Hope Mill workshops at Brimscombe added to the difficulties of the company and in 1925 (at the age of only fifty-four) there was no alternative for Isaac but to wind it up.

(...cont'd)

With the help of a new director, an attempt was made to re-form the company but after a further three years that, too, failed. One final attempt was made to keep manufacturing alive, this time through diversifying output with the production of ventilating equipment on the same site. Boats were still made there but by then it had become a secondary activity. When, in 1930, Isaac Abdela died there was little impetus for the company to continue as it had done. In any case, the Depression years were hardly the time to promote new ventures based on international trade and, as if to mark the demise of the area, the local authority allowed the canal to silt up so that it was no longer useable. It was, in all respects, the end of an era.

New Directions

The Abdelas had left the Mediterranean but the Mediterranean had not left them. As Isaac's story shows, the pull of the sea and the romance of boats was still a potent force. But that would not necessarily carry through to future generations and, to be ahead of the field, it was time to look in new directions.

Shortly after Isaac's only son, Frederick Jacob (generally known as Fred), celebrated his twentieth birthday, the world was plunged into the Great Depression. If for no other reason than the plight of the old economy, it was the right time to move away from Manchester and its traditional industries, and to think twice before investing in international trade. Young Fred proved himself to be nothing if not enterprising and he had a good eye for trends and new ventures. For him a future with promise lay in catering, not in Manchester but in London. People would always want to eat, even (perhaps especially) at a time of economic gloom. The only problem was that there were already some major players in the field, so, to stand a chance of success, he had to be inventive and do something different.

The British had never by then enjoyed a good reputation for their cooking. Although modern diners would later revel in the choice of organic ingredients that were once the norm, by the time they appeared on the table in this earlier period any inherent attraction was lost. Foreigners would mock the presence of tasteless boiled cabbage, of fatty meat swimming in grease, and stodgy puddings with lumpy custard. Of course, there were exceptions but more often than not it was the fare of a factory canteen. It was a question of eating because one had to, rather than by choice. Nor was there, in any case, sufficient disposable income to attract young people and families; eating out was still very much a luxury.

In looking for alternatives, Fred alighted on the new concept of the milk bar. The United States had already pioneered soda fountain bars but it was in Australia that milk bars (the same model as soda bars but with a different product) first took off. Joachim Tavlaidis was a Greek immigrant who opened the first of his chain of Black & White milk bars in Sydney. They sold only milkshakes but in different flavours, the most popular at the start being a banana milk cocktail and what was known as a bootlegger punch (with a dash of rum essence). The addition of ice cream came later.

Milk bars became enormously popular, less because of what they sold and more for their low price and accessibility. They were not like anything else of their kind, with a long counter where customers stood and with very few tables. There was nothing inhibiting about walking in and buying a milk shake and there was no incentive to spend too long in the bar; from the provider's point of view it was all about a quick turnover. It was also a way of bringing in customers who would never have contemplated going to a more formal restaurant. They appealed especially to young people and became something of an icon in youth culture.

Abdela

Modernity Arrives

Fred Abdela saw the opportunity to introduce milk bars in London in the 1930s and, with the brand name of Moo Cow Milk Bars, the first was opened near Victoria Station. There was something very modern about the concept and other branches soon followed. The décor was in light colours, in contrast with the dark greens and browns of more utilitarian eating houses. Open to the street, they were inviting, especially to those venturing into a 'restaurant' for the first time. And because they drew in young people they had a buzz about them that had never been experienced before.

(...cont'd)

As the idea caught on, Hollywood confirmed their hold on the popular imagination. Shots of American youth, exuding a sense of health and vigour, filled the cinema screens in glorious technicolour. Their dowdy counterparts in Europe looked on in wonder at these members of a super race sipping milk shakes and always laughing, with not a care in the world except who was dating who. It helped, too, when the stars in question draped themselves seductively over their orange Oldsmobiles and turquoise Packard convertibles, against the backcloth of a constantly blue sky. Hollywoood was only a milkshake away.

Fred had found a winning formula and it was not surprising that he faced competition. Starting around the same time was another entrepreneur of immigrant stock, Charles Forte. He, too, saw the potential of milk bars and opened his first one in Regent Street. By 1938 there were five in his growing chain and more followed after the war. Forte was a business rival but the two men, Fred and Charles, knew each other and showed a genuine respect for each other's talents.

Having broken into one market, Fred was later lured by another venture that was similarly packed with American imagery, the roadhouse. This was a direct response to what would become the ubiquitous use of the motor car and would typically be sited on a main thoroughfare to and from a nearby city. Fred chose the Great West Road for his own early 1950s venture, seeing it as a 'quick stop' country club where one could sip a fashionable cocktail and get a good meal at a table alongside a heated swimming pool. Design was important too in creating the right effect.

> *Roadhouse promoters wanted to project an image of luxury as much as comfort in a recreational centre replete with the most modern technology and expensive conveniences, especially in the accommodation rooms. For all these reasons, the style chosen most often was the prevailing 1930s architecture. Flat roofs, barren walls, unadorned surfaces, pronounced lines, metal-framed horizontal windows, curved shapes, streamlined counter-tops and chrome characterized the new Modern style.[56]*

Like the earlier milk bars, however, road houses were to have a limited shelf life, their growth interrupted by the Second Word War and never really becoming a feature of the postwar British leisure landscape of the 1950s. They were overtaken in popularity by large pubs with car parks along the arterial roads, a modern version of traditional coaching houses.

Fred could see the limits of roadhouses, and, instead, extended his activities into a number of restaurants within a downtown setting, including one with a resident string orchestra. But far more successful in his business career was the decision to open an industrial bakery, to deliver good-quality patisserie to restaurants around London. He correctly saw an emergent demand for products which individual outlets could not themselves provide. Consequently, each morning a fleet of brightly-coloured Moo Cow vans could be seen in the streets of the capital, always in a hurry to deliver in time for the lunchtime trade. A favourite amongst buyers was the catering-size Black Forest gateau, an emblem of the 1960s and always certain to attract admiring glances.

The bakery, located in Ladbroke Grove, was a masterpiece of planning, and its enticing products hit the market at just the right time. Amongst the main buyers were the new coffee bars, with their juke boxes and live jazz groups, attracting a young generation and nourishing the further development of a modern youth culture. When he was ready to retire, Fred sold the business to one of the country's industrial food giants, having made his own, important contribution to the world of catering at a time of transition.

Professional Choice

For an Englishman, a profession was like a badge, a declaration of belonging, and even if the terms 'trade' or 'occupation' were more loosely defined in the early modern period than they are today, they shaped a person's life, prospects, and identity at least as much as religion.[57]

With some notable exceptions (like the golden age of Jewry in Spain) Jews were habitually denied entry to the professions. There is a mixture of reasons for this. As shown in earlier chapters, their presence in a country was conditional upon performing particular tasks, and living in prescribed locations.

Almost universally, they were treated as aliens, denied access to the inner sanctum of society. And the professions were certainly part of this exclusive realm, enclaves where entry was strictly controlled. It was better that they remained tailors and traders, boat-builders and shipping agents, relying on their own natural wit rather than begging admittance to professions still resistant to newcomers.

But slow though it was, there were at least some signs of progress. In England, even before full emancipation in 1890 finally removed all restrictions for every position in the British Empire, except that of monarch, a select band of Jews (usually from well-established families) were already making a name for themselves in professional posts:

During this [pre-emancipation] period, it was possible for a few Jews from patrician or wealthy merchant families to rise to the highest positions in the Bar or the front rank of the medical profession while retaining a Jewish identity. Examples include Ernest Hart, secretary of the British Medical Association and social reformer, physicians Gustave Schorstein and Bertram Abrahams, as well as lawyers including Sir George Jessel, Master of the Rolls, and Rufus Isaacs, the first Jewish Lord Chief Justice. [58]

These notable individuals, however, were still exceptions rather than the rule and:

... until 1914, the number of Jewish professionals in the UK was small, with no more than 90 or 100 doctors practising in London and perhaps a slightly smaller number of Jewish barristers.[59]

Perhaps because they had been denied entry for so long, the attraction of professional careers assumed great importance in Jewish families. To have a Jewish son who was a doctor or a dentist, a lawyer or accountant was every Jewish mother's dream. In the words of a typical Jewish joke:

A Jewish mother is walking down the street with her two young sons.
A passerby asks her how old the boys are.
'The doctor is three,' the mother answers, 'and the lawyer is two.'

Business was still an obvious path to take but widening the field of opportunities in this way was surely a sign of social acceptance. As it happens, these professions offered ways to be well rewarded too. After all those years of living on the margins of society, it seemed that everything was now coming together. My own relatives are no exception to this general trend and they have produced some notable examples of professionals making good. A leading light in law, for instance, was Judge Jack Abdela, who was born into one of the Sephardi households in Manchester in 1913. His father was Joseph, one of the seven offspring of Elia Abdela, and his mother, Dorothy. As a bright child, Jack gained a place at Manchester Grammar School and later Cambridge University. From there, the doors opened for an illustrious career that saw him preside over a number of high-profile criminal cases of the twentieth century. 'Judge Jack' was widely known in the profession and through legal reports in the broadsheets.

Other family members joined professions like accountancy, medicine, estate development and town planning but, surprisingly, there is no evidence of dentistry. Eschewing the world of business, my own varied path took me from a start as a professional town planner in London, through a subsequent academic career, and, more recently, on an overseas odyssey. I am presently writing this book on an island in the Indian Ocean, a strange place to choose as it is the only place I have known without either a Jewish community or even the historic remnants of a former place of worship. But, then, the diaspora is full of strange stories of chance and opportunity.

From the time that Jews were favoured as physicians in the Spanish courts (pre-expulsion), a career in medicine has been an important aspiration. With its well-regulated entry regulations and lengthy training period, however, it was never easy for an itinerant and often impoverished community to make this possible. Only time and the fulfilment of emancipation, in spirit as well as statute, eventually saw the removal of these barriers, and with a combination of hard work and inherent talent there were no limits to what could be achieved. The example of my cousin, Lawrence Beilin, is an illustrative story.

Hardy

The Long Arm of Moses Maimonides

Maimonides (as he is popularly known) is an extraordinary figure in Jewish history – a quintessential scholar who practiced as a rabbi, philosopher and physician. Everything that he achieved is all the more remarkable when one recognizes that it all happened 800 years ago. What is more, like so many other Jews of that time, he was driven as a young man from place to place, finally settling for most of his life in Cairo. Interesting though he is, one might conjecture that he can surely offer no more than an historical cameo, with little or no relevance to the modern age. In some respects this is true but one question, especially, refuses to go away. Was he a rabbi *and* a philosopher *and* a physician, or was he able to bring these three separate strands together? In particular, how did he reconcile the spirituality of religion with the science of medicine? These are still relevant questions. Is it possible, as Maimonides sought to do, to excel in medicine and yet at the same time remain a devout Jew?

 Fast forward eight centuries and it seems that a contemporary family member, Lawrence Beilin, has offered his own answers. Now an Emeritus Professor and Senior Honorary Research Fellow in the Faculty of Health and Medical Sciences at the University of Western Australia, it is more than four decades since he embarked on what was to become a career-defining journey. No less, his family life was always central to his thinking and his arrival in Perth would change lives across several generations.

Born in England before the Second World War – the only son of Jacob (Jack) Beilin and Josephine (Jo) Hardy – through his own ability and determination, Lawrence charted a direct course to a career in medicine. In spite of keen competition for places, he trained and qualified as a practitioner at King's College Hospital in London. He then undertook postdoctoral training in Los Angeles and then the Postgraduate Medical School in London, before moving in 1968 with the support of his wife, Brenda, to a prestigious appointment in Oxford.

For nine years he held the joint post of First Assistant to the Regius Professor of Medicine at Oxford University and Honorary Consultant Physician at the Radcliffe Infirmary. The experience gained there was unique, and Oxford offered a convivial as well as stimulating setting.

But the time came when he was ready to set up his own department rather than remain for too long in someone else's shadow. An opportunity presented itself when he learned of the intention of the University of Western Australia to re-establish academic activity at the Royal Perth Hospital. It was an opening too good to miss and his appointment to a Chair in Medicine at the university marked the start of a new chapter in his life. Moving to Australia with a young family was no small matter but the decision was taken and Perth became their home of choice. His three sons took well to their new surroundings but Lawrence wanted his parents to be part of the experience too. As a result, they were soon to join the family in Perth, where Jack found work in his previous profession as an optician, continuing in employment until the age of 75. The bringing together of the family was important, not just in terms of practicalities but because this is an essential feature of Jewish custom and practice.

In all respects, the move to Western Australia proved to be an enormous success. In his post, Lawrence himself responded enthusiastically to the professional challenge, gaining an international reputation as a distinguished physician and making a major contribution to the development of medical education and practice – for which, amongst other awards, he was appointed Officer of the Order of Australia in 2003. He has published widely and consistently, over a long period, in the fields of cardio-vascular disease, hypertension, nutrition and blood circulation, attracting numerous citations for his work and invitations to speak at international gatherings. As an Emeritus Professor, and now well into his 80s, he remains active in both research and practice, sharing his knowledge freely with professionals and students alike.

With all the changes and new activities, one might have thought there would be little time to devote to the Jewish community in which he and Brenda found themselves. But that was not the case, and (just as they had done in Oxford) they were soon to be regular attenders of a synagogue in the city. Initially, they joined a Liberal congregation, where their three sons were all bar mitzvah'd. Later they transferred to an Orthodox synagogue, although Lawrence feels he still veers more towards Liberal practice and beliefs, describing himself as a Jewish atheist who nonetheless remains proud of his heritage of Jewish ethics and tradition. With their extended multicultural family Lawrence and Brenda now enjoy more home-based Jewish festive celebrations; and with his strong sense of Jewish identity and history, Lawrence is active in countering anti-Semitism and defending all oppressed minorities.

As a physician, Lawrence practices what he preaches, placing great emphasis on keeping fit. Each morning, he and Brenda swim in the ocean, they walk regularly and are careful with their diets.

(...cont'd)

One cannot help but bring to mind again the example of Maimonides, who never neglected his religion and who saw it as his duty to God to look after his body, just as he would advise others to do. In the words of one scholar on his ideas:

> *Maimonides states that the preservation of one's own health is a sacred duty because 'a perfect body is essential to the proper serving of God'. He takes the position that illness is, for the most part, the result of overindulgence and man's neglect of his own health. He then goes on, in exhaustive detail, to set forth the principles of a healthy life: the importance of food, cleanliness, and self-control. These were principles from which he never deviated in his subsequent medical works.[60]*

Science and religion are not incompatible and it was shown in his writings that this could be clearly explained. Rather than be in conflict they can be seen as a continuum, a source of wholeness in mind and body. Eight hundred years after his death, Maimonides still offers food for thought and a guide to everyday practice that remains remarkably relevant.

Creative Talents

Before about 1850, we don't see much evidence of Jewish creativity in most realms of cultural life. What seems to have changed thereafter is their increasing admission into the institutions of Western culture.[61]

Certainly, when Jews were at last given a voice in mainstream society the lid came off; the repressed energy of generations was released to make its mark in just about every creative pursuit. Writers, artists, musicians, sculptors, actors, film-makers, journalists, broadcasters, not to mention creativity in the sciences, all featured exceptional individuals. The names in a crowded field are legend: Saul Bellow and Franz Kafka; Lucien Freud and Jacob Epstein; Danny Kaye and the Marx Brothers; Gustave Mahler, André Previn, Stan Getz, Leonard Cohen; Albert Einstein and a disproportionate number of other Jewish scientists, including Rita Levi-Montalcini, who were to receive a Nobel Prize.

As an example of creative talent amongst my own ancestors, there is the distinguished record of a distant relative through marriage, Asher Beilin.

Hardy

The Power of the Pen

Asher Beilin (formerly Beylin) and his wife, Zipporah, came to England in 1906 from Kiev via Austria. Widely known as Oscar (rather than Asher), he was the paternal grandfather of my cousin, Lawrence. His was an intellectual journey but he was also active in supporting the Jewish cause in different ways. By the time he arrived in London, he was already well known as a journalist and writer in three languages – Yiddish, Hebrew and English. And through periods of schooling in Switzerland and Germany, he was (like his scholarly father before him) familiar with important currents of European ideas. Both father and son were advocates of Jewish enlightenment, looking beyond conventional Hebrew learning for connections with other cultural traditions. Before he came to England, Oscar had worked with Sholem Aleichem, a renowned Yiddish writer.

For the following quarter of a century, he was based in London, reaching out to a wide variety of publishing outlets. He wrote critical literary treatises, feature essays and current events pieces, and was prolific in writing and translating books, though was mainly active as a journalist and correspondent.[62] Only one of his books was published in English, *Baptism and Other Stories*, dated 1931.

During the First World War he worked in Whitechapel, publicizing the contribution of the Jewish Legion, and between 1920 and 1933 he promoted the work of the Jewish National Fund. In the year that Hitler came to power, Oscar migrated to Palestine with his daughter Hilda; his other daughter, Sylvia, joined them after 1945. He contributed regularly to the Yiddish and Hebrew press and continued to write books, living just long enough to see the formation of the new state of Israel in 1948.

Another example of creative talent in my family is that of Jeffrey Bernerd, a brother of my paternal grandfather, who changed his name from Bernhard Simon when he left England after the First World War to seek fame and fortune in the nascent film industry in Hollywood.

Hardy

'Lights, Camera, Action!'

Jeffrey worked mainly as a producer but he also has credits as an actor and writer.[63] It was a fiercely competitive environment but he stayed the course and it was clear from correspondence that he never looked back. In a letter that he sent from a Beverly Hills address to my father in 1944, he reported:

> *Am very lucky to be out here but get very homesick, it's strange how fate works, it's like a dream to me, often I shake myself to make sure that I am not asleep and that I shall awake to find myself in London.*

His wartime letter was also an opportunity to give some good news about his work:

> *Am happy to say that I have made two big successes. One will be shown in London very soon, its title is 'Women in Bondage', the other is 'Where are your Children?' See them.*

Another highlight of Jeffrey's career was the production of three 'B' movies in the 1940s. 'B' movies (lasting for about an hour) were popular at the time for supplementing the main feature in a cinema and completing an evening's entertainment. Invariably, they were fast-moving with larger-than-life heroes and villains. The titles of his films all indicate how they fitted this bill, with *King of the Bandits*, *Robin Hood of Monterey* and *Forgotten Women*. Sadly, shortly after his name was getting more widely known, he died, in 1950, but if that had to be where better than in iconic Beverley Hills?

At least he knew that his son, Jack, would remain in the business, following very closely in his own footsteps. One difference was that Jack concentrated more on directing films (with a total of thirteen to his credit) but he also produced no fewer than nine and he wrote the screenplay for *West of Carson City*.

A third example comes from the world of photography, a profession where, it seems, Jewish talent excelled.

Moss

Baron's Court

Baron Stirling Henry Nahum was born into the Sephardi community in Manchester in 1906, and is related to the Mosses on my maternal grandmother's side of the family. His father, with an Italian Jewish lineage, had come to England from Libya. Before that, Baron's family roots can be traced back to Spain and then Holland.

Known simply as Baron in his career as a society photographer, he was widely recognized by the great and the good, including the British royal family. He formed a friendly relationship with Prince Philip, the Duke of Edinburgh, who took an interest in what Baron had to say about photography and trusted him as a confidant. When Philip and the then Princess Elizabeth were married in 1947, Baron was commissioned to take colour photos to mark the event. His appointment as a court photographer was assured and in the following years he produced regular portraits of the royal couple.

Before his association with royalty, during the 1930s, Baron was already known for his sensitive understanding and depiction of the world of ballet. As well as using his photos to explore the subject he also wrote about it. His reputation grew and, undoubtedly helped by his acceptance in royal circles, he was much in demand by celebrities of the day.

> *The archetypal English 'gent' in his customary tweeds and brogues, Baron shot everyone who was anyone between 1945 and 1956 – Elizabeth Taylor, Marilyn Monroe, Tito, Franco, Dietrich, to name but a few. His easy-going affable style, together with his great love of life, marked him out from other photographers of his generation and he developed close, personal relationships with a number of his sitters.* [64]

Given the number of commissions that were coming his way, it was a logical step to open a studio with a team of fellow photographers and assistants. This he did in a Mayfair location 1954, just two years before his untimely death in 1956 at the age of fifty.

(...cont'd)

As a sign of his professional esteem, Anthony Armstrong-Jones, first Earl of Snowdon and husband of the queen's sister, Margaret, spent the first year of the studio's history apprenticed to Baron to learn more about photography.

In his relatively short life, Baron made an enduring name for himself in his chosen field. He carved a distinctive path that spoke of his own approach but he was not alone in the Jewish community in advancing the cause of photography. In the words of an historian of the subject:

> [Jews] were prime movers behind nearly all things photographic in Britain until at least the 1970s... They profoundly shaped what came to be known as photojournalism. They were pioneers in applying photography to the fine arts. They were at the cutting edge of collecting, curatorship, the writing of photographic criticism and history, and photographic publishing.[65]

The studio that Baron created continued in business for another twenty years after his death, before further commissions were no longer taken and the archive was donated by a well-wisher to the National Portrait Gallery.

Chapter 5

Jewish Women

From the now largely defunct country clubs in the Catskills to still-lively function rooms in north London, Jews have always loved to make jokes about themselves. Taken out of context, some of the jibes might even seem anti-Semitic, but not within a Jewish gathering.

> *In a restaurant, a table of Jewish women had started on their lunch when their waiter came over.*
> *'Ladies,' he said, 'is anything to your liking?'*

Jewish women are the butt of a fair share of jokes, though probably no more than other groups. If you think women are hard done by, you should spare a thought for the rabbi!

But who *is* a Jewish woman? Is she the harassed driver of that battered Volvo, wearing a woolly hat, with rows of squabbling children along the back seats? Or perhaps she is standing in a group at a wedding, dressed to the nines, adorned with everything that glitters and disdainfully looking the others up and down? Maybe, instead, she is at home in the kitchen, frying fish for the Friday night dinner, the quintessential Jewish mother, fulcrum of the family? Why not, instead, a young Jewish intellectual, with a picture of Rosa Luxemburg over her desk, earnestly trying to explain why Israel veered so quickly from the path of socialism? More likely, though, it is someone just getting on with her life, like any other woman, neither belonging to a single type nor flaunting or denying her Jewishness.

Stereotypes are all, in some respects, slightly ridiculous, trying to fit everyone into a few artificial categories. Life is more complex than that. And yet, to argue against myself, I can see some elements of my family in each of the above. There are features that strike a note of recognition as well as difference. My own mother comes closest to an image of women as home-makers, selfless to a fault, always putting the family first. She never had the kind of kitchen that is now regarded as normal but in her cramped galley she somehow produced dishes that spoke of an evocative past. If she had been given more of a chance, she would have been good at business.

But girls in the Sephardi community where she grew up were not expected to take up a career and, although her parents could have afforded it, a good education in Manchester was denied her. She was assigned a role in the home that was already disappearing.

The fact is that nothing stands still. And one can see, across different generations just how much things have changed for women, especially over the past half century. In the course of this history, it is an unending journey from *traditional* to *modern* but it would be a mistake to suggest that for everyone it has been the same. Many women, through choice as well as custom, are still aligned more closely to traditional roles, while others are unquestionably modern and no different from other women in society. In assessing how closely to general trends the women in our own families have fared, much depends on the availability of the records. Details of their individual histories cannot be traced back far beyond the eighteenth century, and most of the evidence is to be found more recently. It would be fascinating to look at earlier periods too but even over the past couple of hundred years the world has changed in so many ways, and with it the place of women.

Later in this chapter we will look more closely at the story of Rosetta Joseph (née Nathan), who in one sense portrays a traditional model of a Jewish woman, doing what she was supposed to at the time. In another sense, though, she was quietly questioning the boundaries of her restrictions and, in her own way, pushing them outwards by example. We will also look at the case of Lesley Abdela, a cousin and contemporary figure, who has devoted herself to the role of women in society. She is, herself, an entirely modern woman who has lent her own considerable influence to stretching the boundaries of social change. But, first, we need to look at the common starting point for all Jewish women, to see the role they were traditionally assigned and to appreciate just how far they have had to come to make a difference.

Following the Script

It is not good that the man should be alone; I will make him a helper fit for him.[66]

Every Jewish woman knows where to find the rules of engagement and, starting with the Five Books of Moses, the Hebrew bible is a rich store of beliefs as well as instructions. Not much is left to chance and a great deal of what can be done is carefully codified. There are more than six hundred commandments brought together in the Torah and then interpreted and reinterpreted in the Talmud.

Indeed, one does not have to go far into the bible to get a measure of things. The quote at the start of this section is, of course, the first time that Eve comes into our consciousness. And it hardly sets man and woman on an equal footing. Nor does it help that Eve's first act, in succumbing to temptation, is one of weakness. For the rest of history, there is a lot of ground to make up. In fact, most of the bible conveys the same message, of a world where men are the leaders and, with rare exceptions, women are shown in a passive role. An early exception is the prophetess, Deborah (who was also the only female judge mentioned in the bible). She is portrayed as far-sighted and fearless, giving inspiration to the Israelites to defeat the Canaanites and reclaim what is seen as their own land.[67] But Deborah, for all her strengths, is outnumbered by the likes of Moses and David, Solomon and Abraham. In the bible, women can bear children and offer advice to the men but are seldom called on to take a leadership role. They are by no means invisible, yet there are few instances where they can change the course of events. It is, by and large, men who lead armies into battle and who design, build and rebuild the Temple in Jerusalem; it is men who are the priests and intellectuals, the artisans and artists. The great casting director in the sky did few favours for women.

But why was this so? Why were women, from the start, assigned secondary roles? There is surely no inherent reason to treat them as the weaker sex. Rather, it was more a question of assumptions building on assumptions: the hidden idea that God was surely a man, the notion that Eve exemplified the weakness of women, the unquestioned belief (fostered by rabbis who were, of course, male) that it was the task of a man to handle the holy documents in a place of worship. Right up to the present time, nothing illustrates this division more starkly than the sight of women seated in a balcony while men administer the liturgy in their own space below. This particular practice is now restricted to certain synagogues but for most of Jewish history it was the norm.

Women, of course, were enjoined to conform with many things in the same way as men, but there were also requirements and taboos which applied to them alone. It used to be the case that to achieve a *minyan* – the minimum number of Jews assembled for prayer in a synagogue – ten adult males must be present. During the service itself, women were traditionally cast in the role of onlookers. When, for instance, the point is reached when someone in the congregation is asked to read from the Torah, the task was given only to men. The male rabbis who interpreted the rules of prayer also determined that a woman, during menstruation, should not engage in sexual relations with their husband. When their monthly condition ended, they had then to cleanse themselves in ritual waters. In other respects, too, women were expected to dress modestly and to show undying loyalty to their husbands.

The family is at the heart of the Jewish religion and way of life, and women have (traditionally at least) an obligation to bear at least two children to ensure the continuity of the race. As if to make the point, the very first commandment (mitzvah) in the Torah is 'to be fruitful and multiply'. In fact, 'multiply' became the operative word, with no inhibitions to stop at two. Why should they limit themselves, asked the Jewish philosopher, Maimonides, who urged couples to continue to have more children for as long as their health allowed:

> *Although a person has fulfilled the mitzvah of being fruitful and multiplying, he is bound by a Rabbinic commandment not to refrain from being fruitful and multiplying as long as he is physically potent, for anyone who adds a soul to the Jewish people is considered as if he built an entire world.*[68]

It is a commandment that Jewish wives have taken literally and our own family histories contain many examples of this. When, for instance, Jacob Elia Abdela and his wife, Miriam, migrated to Manchester they brought up a family of seven children. That was not an especially large number at the time, and we will see (in the account of Rosetta Nathan that follows) that the number of children counted in double figures was not considered unusual. The average family size has come down considerably, although in Orthodox families they still tend to be numerous, with women bearing a duty to help fill the awesome gap left by the Holocaust.

In what is a remarkably circumscribed world for women, one of the most surprising things is to see that Jewish lineage is derived from the religion of the mother.

> *Motherhood becomes the medium for the continuity of the chosen people. Judaism is a faith founded primarily on familial identity... Anyone born to a Jewish mother is bound, by her motherly love, and by God's motherly love, to the Jewish family and to every other Jew.*[69]

If it were the case that the father is of another religion while the mother is Jewish, it is the mother's religion which counts. This is surprising because it would seem that in all other respects the place of the man is more important; less surprising, though, if one acknowledges that it is the woman who is central to the requirement of perpetuating the race. Admittedly, that could be done through the primogeniture of the man but in this case, unusually, the spotlight is on the woman.

The fact is that so much of what is written is open to interpretation, which was traditionally agreed by generations of exclusively male rabbis. The text that they examined was the word of God, and in theory not open to question, but the reality is different. When there are major changes in society at large, these cannot be ignored by any one part of it. While that does not mean, necessarily, that a Jewish community would have to change in order to be closer to what is going on around it, the case for staying the same has to be convincing. To an extent, a mechanism has been created to allow for this questioning and the possibility of evolution. This mechanism is through the emergence of different branches of the religion. Although there are various categories, for the purpose of this discussion it is enough to point towards opposite ends of the spectrum, to the branches known as Orthodox and Reform. The former, as the name suggests, largely holds firm to traditional beliefs while the latter has seen quite a marked relaxation of rules. Women who belong to the Reform movement can now, for instance, sit alongside men in the synagogue, they can be counted as part of the *minyan*, and they can be called to read from the Torah. What is more, they can serve as a cantor (a traditionally male role) and, importantly, they can be appointed as a rabbi.

It was all very different when Rosetta Nathan shaped her own life.

Moss

Enigmatic Rosetta

A short biographical account of Rosetta Nathan has already been given, tracing her move from the East End to a new life in Australia. Rosetta's story is colourful enough in itself but there is more to it than that as she proved to be a bold and visionary character, who changed the lives of many people around her and quietly created a role model for women in Jewish society. In some ways, she continued a tradition of orthodoxy – giving support to her husband and producing a large family. But it would be a mistake to write her off as just another loyal wife, perpetuating the Jewish race and being the centre of the universe for her many children. She was clearly someone with her own mind and showed remarkable fortitude in difficult conditions.

The dates of Rosetta's life are important – born in 1811 and passing away in 1891; a time when Jewish women would not have expected life to have become any easier. Jews in Europe were engaged in a perpetual struggle for security and acceptance. As she was from an Ashkenazi family, even in the early nineteenth century (before the heaviest incidence of the pogroms) she would have understood only too well what that entailed. Materially, too, the experience of growing up in the deprived conditions of east London would hardly have given hope of anything better.

For most young women in that situation, their future was already mapped out. To add to it all, her father had a record of conviction and transportation, while the man she loved, Moses Joseph, followed suit with his own criminal record and sentence of lifetime exile. There was nothing in Rosetta's background to suggest that she would break the mould.

Perhaps it is a genetic fluke that changes the lives of some people rather than others. Or perhaps it is just a question of luck. Either way, Rosetta's life certainly took an unexpected turn and the worth of her subsequent legacy cannot be understated.

    ℞ For one thing, as a young Jewish woman who was pledged to marry someone of her own kind, she was unwavering in her commitment. When Moses boarded the convict ship in 1827, she was only sixteen years of age. There was no knowing if she would ever see him again but she was determined to do so.

Five years after he left England, she made her own arrangements to buy a ticket and sail to Australia as a free woman. This alone was an incredible thing to do and revealed a woman of exceptional courage.

ℰᴗ On arrival in New South Wales, there was no guarantee that she and Moses would be allowed to marry. His status was that of a prisoner and permission had to be obtained from the Governor of the new colony, which was duly granted. The Governor would have taken into account the exemplary behaviour of Moses since his arrival and then the dedication of his wife-to-be. She would hardly have travelled from one side of the world to the other had she not been serious in intent.

ℰᴗ Between 1833 and 1851 Rosetta bore no fewer than eleven children. If that was a challenge in itself, it was doubly so in the conditions that prevailed in the new colony. Not only was she separated from the rest of her family in England, but all of the pioneer settlers suffered a succession of hardships. It was a tough environment that had to be tamed. Temperatures soared in the southern hemisphere summer months, drought was not uncommon, the rudimentary homes were plagued with flies, and snakes were often to be seen. To add to the problems, supplies from England and other parts of the world were erratic and, until farming could be better established, there was always some uncertainty whether there would be enough to eat. Many of the settlers, who had been forced to relocate from the Old World, were resentful and often unruly. But she and her husband held firm and (even though Moses, on a life sentence, had no choice) they both resolved to stay.

ℰᴗ Rosetta gave all of her children a good start in life and there are plenty of signs of them prospering. Some returned in due course to England but not to the East End. Instead, they lived comfortable, middle-class lives, mainly in London and in one case Liverpool.

ℰᴗ In addition to looking after her own children, she gave active support to her eight siblings, all of whom had been born in east London and, remarkably, all of whom were to follow Rosetta's example and make their own way to Australia. No doubt their father, Nathan, encouraged them to do so (as he had previously done in the case of Rosetta) but having a sister living there would have been a great boost to their confidence.

ℰᴗ Rosetta returned to England towards the end of the 1850s, by then a wealthy woman, and she and Moses were able to live in a smart area of London. But her work was not over and she devoted much of her time and money in her remaining years to generous acts of charity.

Rosetta Nathan was my second great-grandmother, and also that of my cousin, Lesley Abdela. We can only reflect on Rosetta's life with a sense of pride and admiration for what she achieved. She was a good woman who clearly found time for others, and in her own way – by example as well as deed – changed lives for the better. A portrait in her middle years shows elegance as well as warmth, her dark eyes suggesting more than a hint of a smile behind the formal pose. Her expression reveals the strength of character that was so evident in what she did, but it also shows the humanity that she shared so generously with others. There is something almost Mona Lisa-esque about the portrayal, enigmatic to the point of offering an intriguing mix of tradition and modernity. She was certainly an important figure in this family history.

Rewriting the Rule Book

Be realistic, demand the impossible.[70]

For the greater part of Jewish history, tradition shaped the behaviour of women. Their role was clearly defined by word and deed: a role at the heart of home and family. As recently as the nineteenth century, this was still very largely how it was. On the face of it, Rosetta Nathan was a traditionalist, although in important ways she was already looking towards (and helping to shape) a different landscape. The journey from one to the other was not, however, going to happen overnight; it would be a gradual process, with incremental change the order of the day. Obstacles had to be removed; the route was strewn with unwritten assumptions that had become the norm over the years. It was time to question all that had for so long been unquestioned. It was, indeed, time to rewrite the rule book.

Rosetta passed away in 1891. Had she lived into the new century she would have witnessed in England the emergence of the suffragette movement, with calls for women to have the same voting and other rights as men. A little later she would have seen women going to work in factories, filling the gaps left by men who went to fight in the First World War. The national interest led to changes in society that would not otherwise have occurred (or certainly not at that point). There were advances and retreats in the years that followed but the trajectory was consistent. When war broke out again, in 1939, a further impetus for change occurred. Women, as before, were drawn into active roles outside the home, not only contributing to the immediacy of the war effort but also offering their own ideas on what peacetime could bring. There was to be no going back this time and important changes proved irresistible. After the 'people's war' came the 'people's peace'. Education for all and free medical care were important pillars of the new welfare state, although it took several more decades before the many advantages for women of these radical changes in society could be fully realized. To some extent, the 1950s saw a falling back into traditional roles in society but that was just the calm before the storm of the 1960s, when it seemed that everything could at last be questioned. On the agenda this time, not by default but as a conscious movement, was the cause of 'women's liberation'. Demands were at first resisted, if not ridiculed, by male-dominated politicians and the media but in time this resistance, too, gave way to the forces of change.

If the context for this trajectory in the twentieth century could be described in one word, it is 'modernity'. Technology offered the tools to do things in different ways, and society responded (albeit not always with good grace). Modernity was not as eagerly embraced in Britain as in some countries but it was still inevitable. That was not to mean that tradition was swept away indiscriminately; rather, in an effort to please all parties, it was embodied within a modernist shell. A former prime minister of the UK, John Major, for example, invoked nostalgic images to conceal a modern future:

> *Fifty years on from now, Britain will still be the country of long shadows on county [cricket] grounds, warm beer, invincible green suburbs, dog lovers, and – as George Orwell said – old maids bicycling to Holy Communion through the morning mist.*[71]

John Major was right and he was wrong. He was right in that certain traditions would not disappear. But he was wrong in failing to point out that their meaning would change; tradition would in future offer a stage set, a background, rather than drive the essential motor of society. It would become a world of strange contradictions. Pubs, for instance, would be renovated to emphasize their history, while inside there would be conversations about global finance; heritage designs would be commissioned to sell newly-built houses that looked like period counterparts, but equipped with advanced technology; and, in reverse, modern, fitted kitchens would be beyond the wildest dreams of earlier generations, yet still remain largely the preserve of women. New ways were emerging but nothing was yet entirely as it might seem.

Beyond the home environment, women have, quite dramatically, changed the balance of the workforce but successive surveys show that there are still differences in relative pay levels and posts of responsibility. Female students are now as numerous as their male counterparts but what happens when they emerge beyond the protective walls of their universities? There have undoubtedly been enormous changes, and tradition in all spheres has been eroded, but there are still resistant features that prolong past divisions.

To see not only how much has been done to close the gender gap in the case of women, but also how much still needs to be achieved, we turn to another family member, Lesley Abdela. As we will see, she has devoted her career tirelessly to the cause.

Abdela

Boots on the Ground

Lesley comes from a lineage where enterprise and determination were dominant qualities. Rosetta Nathan was her maternal great-great-grandmother; later, grandfather Isaac, starting from scratch, made a name for himself in the business of building ships; and her father, Fred, was innovative and successful in modern forms of catering. But nothing in this background could have prepared Lesley for the particular career she pursued, as an activist, campaigning internationally for women's rights, challenging all that had been taken for granted. In her own words she describes herself as:

> ... a recognized 'boots-on-the-ground' specialist on issues related to women in politics and public life, gender equality, women's rights and peace-building after deadly conflict and have worked in the former Soviet Union and Asia to the Middle East/North Africa and across sub-Saharan Africa.[72]

It is a remarkable career that might not have been possible for a woman – whether Jewish or not – even a generation earlier. Had she grown up, for instance, in the comfortable, Sephardi community of south Manchester in the first half of the twentieth century, her future could have been very different: bridge parties and charity dinners, time spent employing and training domestic staff, and guiding what would probably have been numerous children along correct paths. Instead, following her own interests, she started as an advertising executive in London before focusing on politics, first as a parliamentary researcher and Liberal Party candidate for a seat in the House of Commons. With this challenging experience it was a natural progression to work as a political journalist and lobbyist.

Bright and articulate, full of ideas, Lesley gained a national reputation when in 1980 she founded the 300 Group, a cross-party initiative campaigning for more women in the UK parliament. In one way and another, that was to be at the heart of her activities, not simply in this country but internationally. She was drawn, especially, to the difficulties faced by women in war-torn parts of the world where democracy hardly existed and women barely had a voice.

(...cont'd)

Her calling took her to volatile parts of the world that most people chose to avoid. In the course of her subsequent career, she was to work in more than forty such countries.

Much of her early work followed the fall of the Berlin Wall and the opening of the eastern bloc. Boundaries could now be crossed but the prospect of introducing democratic institutions posed a major challenge, not least of all for women, who – in spite of living in supposedly socialist regimes – had been used to seeing men in charge. Challenges, though, bring their own opportunities and Lesley was quick to see that she could play a part in the evolving tableau. She worked closely with individuals and organizations dedicated to assisting the former communist satellites to successfully make the transition to democratic systems. An early assignment was to be sent as a war correspondent to a besieged enclave in Bosnia, where she interviewed women on how they were coping with the grim situation. This was the first, and by no means the easiest, of a series of frontline 'boots-on-the-ground' encounters. Later she would return, repeatedly, to Kosovo, another part of the former Yugoslavia, to conduct training courses and make links with support agencies. She became well known there and formed close links with various women intent on improving their situation.

In the course of her work, Lesley travelled extensively in other countries in the region, like Poland and Hungary, the Czech Republic and Slovakia, Romania and Bulgaria, conducting workshops and organizing meetings where women could discuss the possibility of a very different future. Her reputation spread and, during this period, she was also invited to undertake projects in a number of countries in Africa, such as Ghana, Nigeria and Tanzania.

Contacts were important and a close connection was established with the British Council, which was itself keen to play a more pro-active role as a mediator and supporter of democratic change. It was a timely relationship and the then Director-General, and also the Chair of that prestigious body, invited her to join the Board. Her presence was much needed as she became only the third woman in a total membership of twenty-eight. It was an important appointment, not least of all because it enabled contacts at the highest level within the UK and also in the many countries where the Council had a presence. As well as providing training programmes, through the various country offices, Lesley was able to personally meet high-level women representatives of governments and local organizations.

The 1990s were frenetic years but, with the support of the British Council and the Foreign Office in London, time was found for Lesley to join an historic, eight-day train journey from Warsaw to Beijing. The train itself was half-a-kilometre long, carrying women from thirty-six countries to a United Nations conference in the Chinese capital.

As the train trundled across the vast plains of Russia, and then through Mongolia and northern China, there were numerous opportunities for one-to-one and small-group discussions. Many of the women had never before had the chance to openly express their views, and Lesley was active throughout the journey in helping to convince them that what they had to say was important. She explained that this would not be just another conference, like they might have attended in the past, where they were required simply to listen to long speeches by male leaders. The world was changing and this time they would be there as active participants in their own right. Their views were important.

Before the Beijing event, a survey was conducted in the UK, asking women what they wanted; the idea was that this could be reported at the conference. Of the ten thousand responses, priorities included 'the replacement of men by women in all the power positions in the world'. One response, in particular, would have struck a familiar chord for campaigners for more democratic politics:

> *An election where all the parties' candidates must be female to redress the balance of the last eighty years' male domination.*[73]

Lesley has shown herself to be totally dedicated to the cause, and in the new century she was even more in demand. The more she did, the more she was asked to do: appearing on radio and television panels, writing articles for international newspapers and magazines, sharing her views and experience with students at universities, and becoming a popular after-dinner speaker at various gatherings. Along the way, her contribution has been appropriately recognized: to name just a few commendations, in the Queen's honours list as an MBE (Member of the Order of the British Empire) in 1990, as the UK Woman of Europe in 1996 for her work in the former eastern bloc, and UK Woman Political Journalist of the Year in 2009.

Lesley has close relationships with her son, Nick (who is especially keen that we produce this book), and her supportive partner, Tim Symonds. As well as her political work, she is also a talented artist.

Chapter 6

Charitable Intentions

It is not uncommon for migrant groups to stay close together and to offer help to those amongst them who might be struggling. Especially when they find themselves in a hostile environment, acts of charity can also be acts of survival. Jewish communities have shown themselves to be no exception in recognizing the need for support. Indeed, charity has been a central part of their existence and 'equal in importance to all other commandments combined'.[74] Nor is it simply a question of providing help; *tzedakah*, the nearest Hebrew word for charity, has a wider meaning related to justice or righteousness. As such, it is at the very heart of what Judaism stands for.

History explains its importance. Jews were 'on the road' for more than two millennia and faced sustained challenges. They were forced to find places to settle and, even where they could make a valuable contribution, they were rarely welcomed by the resident population. Although outright persecution was sporadic it was, more or less, predictable that it would happen at some time. In the face of violent outbreaks, the paths of Jews, from one land to another, were littered with the debris of properties burned and lives lost. Even when they enjoyed long periods of relative stability, they knew that, sooner or later, they would be forced to move again. Typically, they were at first accepted (albeit grudgingly) and then ousted. As we have already seen, this happened, in mediaeval England, in Spain and Portugal, and later in Poland and then Germany. Further to the east, in western Russia Jews were never fully accepted and it is no coincidence that *pogrom* is a word of Slavic origins. Little wonder, Jews would be suspicious of what their respective hosts had to offer, and came to trust only their own kind. They learned to look inwards, seeking ways to strengthen what little they had rather than rely on the actions of outsiders. Helping one another became almost genetic, a constant feature of Jewish communities throughout the diaspora. Acts of charity transcended national boundaries, occurring wherever they were. Such acts were not incidental to their lives but central.

Charitable acts took various forms in different times and places, but the general pattern was remarkably consistent. First and foremost, charity was directed to helping the poorest amongst them; second, it was always essential to ensure that religious practice could be properly observed across the whole community; third, there was support for a variety of 'good causes', including donations to support non-Jewish interests in their county of adoption; and, finally, money was given to assist the Zionist movement and, after 1948, the fledgling state of Israel. Examples can be found of how different family members contributed to each of these.

Helping the Poor

[New homes] constitute the greatest of all available means for improving the condition, physical, moral, and social of the Jewish poor.[75]

Housing was an important focus for charitable intervention but by no means the only one. The poor needed help in many forms and a profusion of agencies emerged to cater for their diverse needs. From the middle of the nineteenth century, for instance, there was great concern about conditions in the Ashkenazi community in north Manchester. In response, the area saw the growth of dedicated organizations like the Children's Holiday Home; the Jewish Home for Aged & Needy Jews; the Hebrew Bread, Meat, & Coal Society; and the Soup Kitchen for the Jewish Poor. The foundation of a Manchester arm of the London-based Jewish Board of Guardians helped to give direction to the various activities designed to bring relief to those on the very margins of their community. [76]

But, in terms of scale and public attention, there was nowhere to compare with the congested neighbourhoods just beyond the eastern borders of the City of London. Towards the end of the nineteenth century, it seemed that the influx of new migrants would never stop. It was apparent to richer members of Jewish society that, for both humanitarian and political reasons, the situation could not be allowed to continue. Not only was urgent help needed to assist the newcomers in finding decent places to live, but also, if the situation was left to fester, it could fuel the fires of anti-Semitism. People would be quick to blame the immigrants for a shortage of housing, for taking jobs and for spreading disease. Self-interest, therefore, as well as altruism was a motive for intervention.

In response, the self-appointed aristocracy of Jewish society, who had been in the country for a generation or more and were respected by gentile leaders as well as their own kind, took it upon themselves to initiate improvement projects. The problem of sub-standard housing across England as a whole was already the subject of national legislation but the matter would not wait for the wheels of officialdom to turn. A committee was formed, with Lord Rothschild at the helm, and funds were raised for model housing that would balance fair rents with a modest return on capital investment: hence the term '4 per cent philanthropy'.[77] An inauspicious site in Spitalfields, surrounded by notorious slums, was cleared as a prelude to reconstruction. Yet, even with the efforts of an able and influential committee, it took several years before the completion of what were to be known as the Rothschild Buildings.[78] Intended primarily for families of Jewish artisans, this became a landmark development, an emblem for philanthropy.

For those who moved into the model housing in 1887, it was almost as if they had stepped into the Promised Land.[79] The buildings took their first tenants when demand was at its highest, and until the 1970s (by which time the development had long ceased to serve its original purpose) the 5000 men, women and children who lived there at the height of its popularity were almost exclusively Jewish. They were also unmistakably foreign, with their own distinctive dress, language, and ways of cooking. In its early years, it would have felt more like stepping into a ghetto in eastern Europe than a neighbourhood just a short walk away from the financial hub of the British Empire.

For those left behind, however – the poorest of all, who could not afford even the fairly-priced rents of the Rothschild Buildings – there was no respite. The belief was that accommodation vacated in favour of the new housing would help to relieve the situation; it would offer extra rooms for the less fortunate and, with more housing on the market, rents would start to fall. In fact, so long as there was a steady stream of newcomers into the area there was no chance of lower rents and the plight of the most impoverished in Jewish society remained dire. Until they could improve their own lot, the only assistance available was in the form of poor relief, administered by a special body established in 1859: the Board of Guardians for the Relief of the Jewish Poor. This dedicated channel of assistance was deemed essential as the public system of allocating paupers to special accommodation made no allowance for Jewish forms of religious observance. Acts of charity became a lifeline for the newly widowed, for children left as orphans, and families trying to survive while their breadwinner was serving time in prison. There were tragic stories but Isaac Zangwill, observing conditions in the streets that he personally knew so well, could always be relied on to find a way to soften the edges, even of pathos:

> *… these poor Jews were rich in all the virtues, devout yet tolerant, and strong in their reliance on Faith, Hope, and more especially Charity.*[80]

Reliance on charity was simply part and parcel of community life and Zangwill urged that there was nothing to be ashamed about. Beggars and donors alike each had a role to play; one need not feel inferior nor the other superior.

> *Like all genuine philanthropists, he did not look for gratitude. He felt that virtue was its own reward, especially when he sat in Sabbath vesture at the head of his table on Friday nights, and thanked God in an operatic aria for the white cotton table-cloth and the fried sprats.*[81]

Fried sprats, it would seem, were a levelling influence. Givers and takers were in the same community; there were rich and poor and each knew what was expected:

> *As for the rich, they gave charity unscrupulously… The Takif, or man of substance, was as accustomed to the palm of the mendicant outside the Great Synagogue as to the rattling pyx within. They lived in Bury Street, and Prescott Street, and Finsbury – these aristocrats of the Ghetto – in mansions that are now but congeries of 'apartments'. Few relations had they with Belgravia, but many with Petticoat Lane and the Great Shool, the stately old synagogue which has always been illuminated by candles and still refuses all modern light.*[82]

Charitable disbursements went hand in hand with improved housing, the former for those most in need and the latter for an artisanal class. In time, though, the pattern of care widened, reflecting new circumstances and changing demands. Two things happened. One was that, over a period, some members of the original community improved their own standing and chose to move, under their own steam, to more amenable surroundings. They no longer looked to charities to help them do this. The other was that, through a series of reforms, the state provided a safety net for all of its citizens. Progress in this respect was incremental, culminating after 1945 in a fully-fledged welfare state; and, even after that, measures were added and benefits enhanced. Did this mean that there was no longer a need for a dedicated body to assist the Jewish community? The answer to that is 'no' and throughout the twentieth century, and into the present one, the Jewish Board of Guardians has remained active.

The Guardians endowed a legacy of philanthropy which, although the focus of interests changed, was to make a lasting contribution. Illustrating shifts in emphasis, in terms of providing housing it became less a case of catering for the poor and more one of meeting special needs. More attention could be paid to specialist education, health and general welfare projects, as well as supporting women in their own campaign for greater recognition and new opportunities to better themselves. There is also, for instance, a network of Jewish care homes, often named after their benefactors, which can offer its residents everything from kosher food to an in-house synagogue. It is an important (although invariably expensive) option for the elderly, who welcome the assurance that many of the things they have taken for granted in the course of their lives can be continued.

A further change came during the 1990s, with a merger of the Board of Guardians with other charities in the UK to form a new body, Jewish Care. An annual directory points to more than 500 Jewish organizations, encompassing a wide range of causes and activities, ranging from disabilities to volunteering, discussion groups to respite care. The spectrum mirrors that for people of all religions, the main difference being that it allows members of the same faith and culture to share their difficulties and find a way forward that suits them best.

As an example of private philanthropy amongst my own relatives, I can return once again to the path taken by Moses and Rosetta Joseph. Their experience was, indeed, a classic story of giving back. Coming from related families in the East End, they both experienced firsthand the effects of extreme poverty and the general state of deprivation around them. This obviously weighed heavily in their minds and, when their own situation improved, they were not slow to look for ways to help others. It might have helped that the couple knew not only about poverty but also of charity; the one went hand in hand with the other.

Moss

Building a New Community, Remembering the Old

As we already know, Moses Joseph arrived in Australia in chains but, through dint of hard work and business acumen, in a remarkably short period he became a very wealthy man. Moreover, his standing in society was enhanced when, first, his life sentence was made conditional upon good behaviour, and then, in 1848, he was given an unconditional pardon. He was by then, officially, a respectable member of society but even before that he had seen fit to devote time and money to giving something back to the community that had brought him good fortune. As the Australian historian, Suzanne Rutland, has shown:

He used his commercial success to build Sydney's Jewish community. Joseph served on the committee that bought land on York Street in Sydney in 1841 for the purpose of building the first synagogue in Australia, which was opened in 1844. He was president of the Sydney congregation for five years and he also worked to establish the first Jewish school in Sydney, the Sydney Hebrew Academy, in 1846.[83]

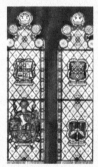

Moses also helped to finance Australia's first seat of higher learning, the University of Sydney. And it was in that connection that his contribution caught the attention of Dr Rutland. Her interest was aroused by a stained-glass window which, it appears, Joseph had donated to the newly-established university in 1857. The window shows not only his name but also, in Hebrew, the word 'Yerushalayim' (Jerusalem). As all the other windows were donated by members of the British aristocracy, the observant historian could not help but ask who was responsible for this.

Perhaps Moses and Rosetta felt by then that their work was done in Australia. They had both shaken off any residue of criminal behavior and succeeded in everything they did – bringing up their own family, helping other family members who joined them as free settlers, building a very successful business empire, and contributing to the establishment and welfare of a Jewish community in Sydney. With this behind them, in 1870 they returned to London. But still their charitable work was not finished and funds were donated for the Jews' School in Stepney and other Jewish primary schools in the deprived part of London where it had all started.

Religious Zeal

They dropped in, mostly in their workaday garments and grime, and rumbled and roared with a zeal that shook the window-panes... [84]

No Jewish community would be complete without its own place of worship, yet there are many Jews (myself included) for whom the synagogue is not the centre of the universe. In the words of one like-minded observer, confronting this paradox:

I don't go to the temple on high holy days, but I'm proud to be Jewish. [85]

It is something of a conundrum that one can be Jewish but rarely, if ever, visit a synagogue – expressed in a typically wry tone by Howard Jacobson:

I was brought up a Jew but, you know, that way of being Jewish – the New York way. We were stomach Jews; we were Jewish-joke Jews. We were bagel Jews. We didn't go to synagogue. I'm frightened of synagogues to this day. [86]

Jews, of course, are a mixed bunch and even 'bagel Jews' may also be seen in *shul*. For all this diversity of traditions and practices, it is fair to accept that a mainstream view would put the synagogue in pride of place in any community. Moreover, arriving, as they did, from different countries and speaking different languages, it was rarely the case that a single synagogue could serve everyone in the same way. Ingenuity was the order of the day and everything was done to cater for all needs, even if the accommodation itself was rudimentary. When they first arrived in the East End, this would often comprise a cramped room for prayer and small gatherings, a place known as a *shtiebel*. The room will have been divided into two:

The rear partitioned off for the use of bewigged, heavy jawed women who might not sit with the men lest they should fascinate their thoughts away from things spiritual... two and often three times a day [they came] to batter the gates of heaven and to listen to sermons more exegetical than ethical. [87]

In time, as communities became better established, it was thought that a synagogue should reflect an element of financial sacrifice and grandeur fit for the purpose, as well as being a place to give vent to religious zeal. As a result, the buildings were invariably architect-designed and contained features that gave pride to the founders. The funds, of course, had to be found within the community. Because of the importance attached to the synagogue, and the sure knowledge that the state could not be asked to provide the necessary resources to build it, Jewish communities themselves have always seen it as their own responsibility. As such, this has been one of the most consistent objects of charity and philanthropy. Wealthy sponsors have been an important source of funding, whether through securing suitable land or assisting in construction. Subsequent costs of operating a synagogue are then largely met through dues paid by members of the congregation.

Moss

Spreading the Word

It is a matter of pride that one of my distant ancestors, Rabbi Dr John Levi of Melbourne could write that 'almost every Jewish community in eastern Australia and New Zealand came into being because of Moses and Rosetta'.[88] Not only the heads of the Joseph and Nathan families, but also other members, were enormously influential in widening the network of Jewish communities to serve new locations in Australia and New Zealand. The record of these related families was pivotal in establishing synagogues and, invariably, taking on the important role of president.

Louis Nathan (my third great-uncle) settled in Hobart, Tasmania, in 1834. Eight years later he was in a position to lay the foundation stone for the first synagogue in the state, on Argyle Street, and on its consecration he became the founding president. Another 'first' was marked by Solomon Benjamin, husband of my third great-aunt, who, with two of his brothers, set up in business in Melbourne. With nowhere officially to worship, he made available space in his own home, where a full *minyan* participated in the first Jewish service in the state of Victoria. In the following year, a foundation stone was laid and Solomon acted as treasurer in the formative years of building a dedicated place of worship, and then serving as its first president.

Just a few years later, in 1851, another relative, Moses Moss (also a third great-uncle), settled in Sydney (following an earlier spell in Tasmania). He, too, was to earn a deserved reputation as a driving force in the management of synagogue affairs and a supporter of numerous charities. In a eulogy at his funeral in 1883, it was said that:

> *...before he was for many years chief warden and treasurer of the Synagogue, and would willingly have served it in any capacity in which the suffrages of its members would have placed him. He was a liberal contributor to its funds, and would have served it day and night... He was a member for years of the committee of the Philanthropical Society, and was also associated with day and sabbath schools, and also was on the committee of the Randwick and Benevolent Asylums, and I may say in all sincerity that no appeal was ever made to him but met with a ready response.*[89]

 A further example of largesse came from another relative by marriage, by the name of George Judah Cohen. His significance is indicated in an obituary in *The Jewish Chronicle* in 1937, in which he is acknowledged as no less than the 'grand old man of Australian Jewry'. It was recorded that George had been a member of the Board of Management of the Great Synagogue, Sydney, for over fifty years, was President of the Congregation about fourteen times and several times its Vice-President. He was an active charitable worker in the local community of which he was one of the earliest members. When he inherited a fortune from an uncle in Liverpool, he devoted the money to charitable purposes in the north of England. He also dedicated land to the City of West Maitland, New South Wales, in order to allow the council to extend a park. In appreciation of the gift, the West Maitland Council decided to call it Cohen Park.

Back in England, later in the same century, the Sephardi community in Manchester can offer examples of funding a variety of synagogues to serve the needs of different sections of their congregation. Some members of the Abdela family were to play their own part. Moreover, associated with the importance attached to the synagogue as a focal point for Judaism is the appointment of senior members of the community to ensure that standards were maintained and the religious objects of the place of workshop met. Of all the posts in this context, that of president was clearly the most prestigious, going beyond religious responsibilities to assume a *de facto* role as community leader.

Abdela

Webs of Worship

Jacob Elia Abdela, who brought his family from Corfu to Manchester in the mid-1870s, had the distinction of previously serving as President of the Greek synagogue on the Ionian island. From the outset, therefore, it can be assumed that he was already regarded as a committed member of the Jewish community. When they arrived in Manchester, the Abdelas were one of a number of families from Corfu and nearby Arta, together comprising the largest element of the new Sephardi gathering.

This familiarity with each other would undoubtedly have eased the process of settling in. It was an opportune time to arrive for another reason too. Just a few years before, a decision had been taken to build a separate synagogue for the Sephardi congregation (who, until then, were invited to share the Ashkenazi place of worship in the northern part of the city). The Abdelas could hardly have been far from the process of completing the new synagogue and helping to attract its own congregation, many coming originally from those parts of the Mediterranean they all knew so well. My mother recalled that her father and brother attended synagogue regularly but (as was customary at the time) the women of the household were less involved.

The development of new synagogues in the city has already been described in an earlier chapter. By the end of the nineteenth century, the number reached thirty and each generated its own constellation of religious and social activities. Additionally, from as early as 1842, a Jewish school was established, with a roll of 800 boys and girls by 1904. There were also 700 infants attached to the school.

Gilded Altruism

The sources of altruism go deep into our evolutionary past.[90]

Research suggests that Jews are more likely to donate to a charity than the general population.[91] Of course, that takes no account of how much is donated but, in itself, the very act of giving to good causes is a trait that every Jew will recognize. It is part and parcel of Jewish life.

Nothing, however, happens on its own and in every Jewish community there will be individuals who are the 'charity doers', the ones who organize house-to-house collections, ensure that important dates are remembered, send notices to the press, and arrange special fund-raising events. These are usually shared duties and some individuals gain a reputation for their reliable handling of particular tasks. Additionally, some ways of raising money are more popular than others. Thus, in looking back at the involvement of my own relatives, one can see – especially amongst the better-off family members – that a favourite activity is a charity gala evening. Although this has become something of an institution across society as a whole, there is no doubt that Jews, especially, love to dress up and get together with friends and family, and eat and drink well during the evening, not to mention the highlight – a cabaret featuring a performer telling Jewish jokes. If this is doubted, a quick search of Google images will show that gala events remain as much a part of the annual charity calendar as ever. This, indeed, is charity in a gilded cage.

To succeed most of all, it helps if the invitation to attend such an event comes from a wealthy individual who can attract others in a similar position. So much the better if the event is held in a location where wealth can most easily be assured. Where better, for example than the iconic setting of Monte Carlo? This is where Dora Abdela spent the later years of her life and earned a deserved reputation for her outstanding work for good causes in that community. Her story, from a modest start in Manchester, is one that must be told.

Abdela

From Manchester to Monte Carlo

Suvi was the oldest son of my great-grandfather, Jacob Elia Abdela. Born in Corfu, Suvi was brought to Manchester as a boy. He grew up in the emergent Sephardi community and subsequently entered the world of business. 'Marrying out' was not common at that time, but love knows no boundaries and in 1894 he married a young Christian woman, Dora Inez Overend. Dora's father was a potato merchant and, when he died, her mother rented rooms, mainly, it seems, to Jewish immigrants looking for business opportunities before deciding whether to settle in England.

By all accounts it was a successful marriage, taking the couple into social circles that each of them might not otherwise have known. Over the coming years, Suvi consolidated his business interests, becoming a wealthy man, before the couple left Manchester to live in Monte Carlo. The casino town on the French Riviera was at the height of its exotic reputation in the early decades of the twentieth century, a reputation enhanced by its portrayal in some of Hollywood's first full-length films. But, after forty years together, Suvi died, leaving Dora to decide what to do with the rest of her life.

An immediate outcome was that in 1938 she booked a ticket to join the Canadian Pacific company's liner, the 'Empress of Britain', on a world cruise. It was a luxurious way to travel and Dora's name is listed in a presentation brochure with the names of all of the passengers (or, as they were more decorously called, 'members'). No doubt, with ball gowns unpacked and a good supply of personal jewellery set aside, there was a voluminous pile of luggage to store in the hold during the voyage. Only the name of Agatha Christie was missing, not to mention the murder of one of the members. For four months, the floating hotel was at sea, calling along the way at such places as Haifa and Honolulu, Bangkok and Batavia, before berthing in New York, where Dora joined a transatlantic liner to take her back to Europe and her home in Monaco.

Then, in the following year, came the war, when Dora embarked on a new venture, using some of her riches to offer allied naval officers a luxurious venue where they could relax over tea or at drinks parties. Monte Carlo was at the time a hub for rich and influential individuals and she came to know well the charismatic ruler of the Principality of Monaco, Prince Rainier.

Lesley Abdela recalls as a child being taken by her parents to the South of France to visit Aunt Dora. 'She was always immaculately dressed in silk dresses with large Edwardian-style hats. The last time I went to visit I was eight years old – she sent across delicious, home-baked, Lancashire-style rice puddings to the Hotel Metropole, where waiters wearing white cotton gloves carried them on a silver tray for my supper.'

Dora gave generously to a variety of charities and would respond to requests from the Prince to sit on various committees. Her work became widely recognized and in 1957 she was the proud subject of the following notice:

CENTRAL CHANCERY OF THE ORDERS OF KNIGHTHOOD.
St. James's Palace, S.W.I. 13th June, 1957.
The QUEEN has been graciously pleased, on the occasion of the Celebration of Her Majesty's Birthday, to give orders for the following promotions in, and appointments to, the Most Excellent Order of the British Empire:
To be Ordinary Officers of the Civil Division of the said Most Excellent Order:
Dora, Mrs. ABDELA, British subject resident in Monaco.

Dora lived for another five years, passing away at the grand age of 93. She had lived a full life that took her far from her roots in the grimy environment of north Manchester.

Funding the Homeland

Israel was not created in order to disappear.[92]

Charity is, by and large, a fairly uncontentious activity. After all, who can reasonably question the act of giving? Occasionally, there might be questions about whether one organization or another should receive funds, or even whether the dubious reputation of a particular donor is in the best interests of the cause. But no-one would dispute the rightness of giving, say, to a home for the elderly or a cancer-care clinic. Only in one area – the allocation of funds to the State of Israel – are questions consistently asked. Why should this be?

Towards the end of the nineteenth century, the newly-formed Zionist movement attracted financial assistance from various sources. It seemed to an increasing number of supporters that the creation of a Jewish homeland was the logical outcome of the diaspora, bringing to an end the constant search for a secure place to live and call one's own. In the face of repeated persecutions wherever they went, it was surely time to settle within a land that had acquired almost mythical status. For the next half century, the campaign gathered pace, although it was not until after the Second World War that the international community allowed the planned state to be born. In the aftermath of the Holocaust, a groundswell of support could no longer be resisted. Especially in the UK and the US, Jewish charities responded quickly to give whatever support they could to assist the survival and development of this modern embodiment of the age-old idea of the Promised Land. This charitable commitment has continued to the present day, although not at the same intensity. In more recent years, some of the initial enthusiasm has waned. Various reasons are offered, including a deepening divide between more liberal-minded Jews in the US and Europe, discouraged by increasingly conservative policies in Israel.[93] Yet this dip should not be overstated. The peak of giving to Israel may well have passed but it remains very significant; on the American agenda, the largest source of charitable funding, it still attracts more money than any other Jewish cause.[94]

Most support for Israel now comes from the Orthodox arm of Judaism, where it is, in effect, mandatory to give to the Promised Land. And some of the original charities in this field remain as active as ever. The Jewish National Fund in the UK, for instance, dates from the early days of Zionism and over the years has directed funds to numerous projects. Its record in the post-1948 period is nothing if not impressive. In its own words, it is 'an environmental and humanitarian trail-blazer':

> *... planting in excess of 240 million trees; building more than 210 reservoirs and dams; developing over 250,000 acres of land; creating more than 1000 parks and providing crucial infrastructure*

and humanitarian support to over 1000 communities.[95]

Presently, the focus of its work is on helping to see the development of the Negev, the largely desert region in the south of the country.

It would be wrong to suggest that all of this has somehow passed by my own family. I recall, in the early days of the new nation, listening to conversations which were full of admiration and pride for what was being achieved. In the aftermath of the Second World War, there was an enormous store of goodwill. And there were invariably collections and opportunities to sponsor particular projects. No doubt, too, prayers were said in the synagogues and at home on Friday evenings to bless the pioneers. But that, I believe, is as far as it went amongst my relatives. The fact is that the majority of Jews in the UK, and even more so in the US, were content to offer money and moral support but in other respects were not persuaded to set out on another journey to a new land. The prospect of taming the arid landscape, surrounded by hostile neighbours, was clearly not sufficiently appealing for them to leave behind the settled existence that they had at last found. So, through various charities, the money kept flowing but most people stayed where they were, my family included.

Chapter 7

Civis Britannicus Sum

Immigrants inherently face a moral dilemma. On the one hand, there will be relief that they have been offered a new homeland; on the other hand, does that mean they have to discard their own culture in the process? Are immigrants expected to demonstrate gratitude and total loyalty to their country of adoption? Is assimilation part of the deal? Or can they find a way to be loyal to both – to their past as well as their new culture?

For Jews, constantly on the move, this has been a perennial issue, though in many cases there has not been a choice. The matter will already have been decided for them. Thus, in the eleventh century when Jews saw an opportunity to settle in England, following its conquest by William I, there was no expectation that they should feel either gratitude or loyalty. They were encouraged to follow the new king to England so that they could provide money-lending services to assist the workings of the new economy. In order to be close to trade, they tended to live in small groups in market towns. If there were several families and single men in one place it would not be uncommon for them to live in the same street or in a cluster of adjoining houses. Their presence might later be marked with a place name like 'Jewry'. Although they were not forced to live in a particular part of town, they invariably chose to do so for reasons of security.

So long as they paid their taxes in good time, that was all the loyalty that was asked of them. The king valued the additional revenue they generated and offered them some form of protection in return. Yet their position was always precarious; the local population could turn on them at a whim, causing not only harm to body and property but also a pretext for expulsion. They were regarded as 'semi-aliens, growing rich as usurers, and observing strange customs'; as such, 'they occupied in the twelfth century a position that was fraught with danger'.[96]

And across Europe it was a similar story, with Jews very largely accepted on sufferance and tolerated only so long as they performed useful tasks for the state. As we have seen in previous chapters, more often than not they were confined to a designated area and prohibited from certain occupations, as well as being forbidden to own land. If they were wise, they kept their heads down and hoped they would be allowed to live in peace. In those circumstances, questions of loyalty did not arise; survival was all that mattered. Ironically, in Germany, where Jews became well integrated, playing an active part in all aspects of the cultural and economic life of the newly unified country, this was to count for nothing. They thought they were serving the nation and all they had asked for in return was acceptance. But that was not to be forthcoming and, ultimately, the only response of the Fatherland was to send the Jewish population to the camps.

Questions of Loyalty

Thou hast given us home and freedom, Mother England.[97]

Could immigrant Jews ever feel a part of the country they came to? Their hearts still yearned for a distant, almost mythical, land they never expected to see. They spoke different languages and brought with them religious and cultural practices that were a world apart from those of their new hosts. Wherever they lived, their background was so different. Many of those who came to England in large numbers towards the end of the nineteenth century had grown up in the *shtetls* of western Russia or earned their living in Baltic towns, learning their trade as tailors and glaziers, furriers and pickle merchants. Could England ever be anything more than another place of temporary refuge, a country where they might carve out a niche before being forced to move on again? That was all they had expected in the past but this time there were at least some grounds for hope of something more.

Apart from a lingering suspicion of Jews as an alien group in an essentially Christian country, there was no immediate threat of violence. Especially for those who had fled the pogroms of eastern Europe, this must have come as an enormous relief. They were free to pick up their various trades and engage in buying and selling, things they had shown themselves to be good at. The main stumbling block – which initially affected only a minority of the migrants – was in the field of civil offices, for which nominees were required to deliver an oath, not simply to God but to do so in the name of Christianity. Unless they agreed to that, they could not become, say, a member of parliament or a city mayor. Jews were also largely precluded from entering a university. A very few entered the hallowed ground of

Oxford and Cambridge, but new opportunities presented themselves through the University of London, which was avowedly secular.

Advocates of the Jewish cause in parliament to remove the remaining barriers to their advancement met stiff opposition but, fortunately, the reformers persisted. One worthy champion was the man of letters, Thomas Macaulay, who, during the 1830s, repeatedly argued that Jews should be given the same rights as other citizens.

> *Let us do justice to them. Let us open to them the door of the House of Commons. Let us open to them every career in which ability and energy can be displayed. Till we have done this, let us not presume to say that there is no genius among the countrymen of Isaiah, no heroism among the descendants of the Maccabees.*[98]

Yet, in spite of the humanitarian as well as libertarian case that was made so eloquently, it was to be more than half a century before the last of the formal barriers came down. Apart from meeting political resistance, the campaign for what was called 'emancipation' was not concerted, attracting criticism that it was led half-heartedly by the Jewish elite, who were reluctant to upset the delicate social balance they had built. In any case, with something like half of all Jews in England experiencing poverty, winning a seat in the House of Commons or opening a shop in the City of London was hardly seen by them as a priority.[99] It was unlikely that they even thought much about it. But emancipation came eventually, with the final piece of legislation put in place in 1890. Certainly, by the last quarter of the nineteenth century, when so many new migrants arrived, Jews were at last free to advance on merit. Numbers were not large to start with but the most talented and ambitious were able to take advantage of new opportunities for careers in politics and the professions (especially medicine and the law). Meanwhile, there were few, if any, remaining obstacles in the way of successful careers in commerce and new forms of retail trade.

On balance, Jews in England proved to be good citizens. Exceptions can always be found but these are greatly outweighed by an obvious sense of loyalty and adherence to the law of the country of their adoption. They appreciated the freedom granted to practice their own religion and to continue some of the old traditions, but they have never sought to usurp the conventions of their new society. It helped that there were already established Jewish families in England and, as mentioned earlier, Disraeli was a shining example for them all. But it was to be another British prime minister, a quarter of a century before, who really changed the rules of the game in their favour.

In the middle of the nineteenth century, Lord Palmerston, an English aristocrat through and through, established an important principle for the country's foreign policy that would not have escaped the notice of incoming Jews. In fact, the pretext for this new initiative was a blatant case of anti-Semitism by the Greek government, which refused to compensate a British citizen whose property was damaged by anti-Jewish riots in Athens. Don Pacifico, a Jew born in Gibraltar, was a British citizen and, having failed to receive justice through the Greek courts, he appealed to the British government for help. His was not the only claim outstanding in Greece, as another British national had failed to extract any payment for land appropriated for a section of the royal palace gardens in Athens.

Palmerston's response was decisive and unexpected (even amongst his fellow politicians), introducing a new principle to underscore foreign policy in the years to come. In arriving at his decision, he invoked the Roman declaration, *Civis Romanus Sum* – I am a Roman Citizen – adapting it to guarantee the safety and protection of British citizens, whoever they were and wherever they might be. To back his words, Palmerston dispatched gunboats of the Royal Navy to blockade Greek ports until the claims of the two British citizens were met. The strategy was henceforth known as gunboat diplomacy and, though effective at the time, it would last for only as long as Britannia ruled the waves. For incoming Jews, it is hard to imagine a more stirring recognition of their worth. First, of course, they had to be awarded citizenship but, once that was done, they would find themselves in the unprecedented position of being members of a protected rather than a beleaguered race. Don Pacifico's claim was not cast aside because he was Jewish but, instead, pursued with the full might of the Royal Navy because he was British.

It would be trite to suggest that Jews subsequently showed their loyalty because of this one aspect of foreign policy, but it would certainly have done no harm. Any suggestion that Jews could not be loyal to both their country of adoption and also to the Zionist call for a return to the Promised Land, was rebutted through experience. When called to arms, Jews were never slow to enlist and to do their duty. Each year, for instance, when the country remembers its dead in two world wars and other conflicts, Jewish ex-servicemen and women are part of the procession that makes its way along Whitehall, past the Cenotaph where wreaths are laid. The event takes place on the Sunday closest to the time and date when the First World War was concluded, at the eleventh hour of the eleventh day of the eleventh month. On the following Sunday, Jewish ex-servicemen and women alone march again to remember their own losses. Being British and also Jewish has never caused a problem of identity.

There are many instances of my own relatives stepping forward to serve the country in times of war and, in some cases, paying the ultimate price. In 1914, outside the offices of the *The Jewish Chronicle* hung a banner, with the words: 'England has been all she could be to Jews. Jews will be all they can be to England'. Of course, there would have been doubts amongst some about leaving their families in order to go away and fight, as there would be in any community at a time of war. But when it was time to enlist, there was no shortage of volunteers.

Goodman/Moss

'We Were There Too'

The above is the title of a recent exhibition of photos of Jews in the First World War,[100] but it also serves the purpose of making the important point that Jews were part of the national effort, contributing to victory.

Prominent amongst my relatives was Simon duParc Abrahams (married to Matilda 'Trixie' Goodman, sister of my paternal grandmother). He enlisted a year before the outbreak of war, serving initially with the 2nd London Division T & S Column and transferring in 1916 to the Royal Army Service Corps. He sustained an injury (believed to be from shrapnel), which left him with a limp for the rest of his life. For his service (like others who emerged at the end of the conflagration) he received a Victory Medal and British War Medal.

Amongst the many other relatives who can record active service were members of the Moss lineage, and their related kinsfolk from the Joseph and Nathan families.

(...cont'd)

For instance, there was Victor Alfred Moss, a corporal in the Infantry Unit of the Honorable Artillery Company; Percy Lawrence Moss, who had the special distinction of serving in both world wars, before being killed in action in the latter; and Hector Albert Moss, who joined the Duke of Cambridge's Own (Middlesex Regiment) 7th Battalion, and died in battle in the fields of Picardy in October 1916.

There are other Mosses who could be mentioned, and the closely related Josephs and Nathans too, who had long before branched out to make their fortunes in Australia. Both Horace Maharatta Joseph and Arthur Joseph Nathan, for instance, fought in the First World War with the Australian Army.

Because of the horrors it gave rise to and the sheer scale of the conflict, the First World War was declared to be the war to end all wars. But, of course, it was not, and little more than twenty years later the first shots were fired in a new global conflict. Once again, members of our families left 'civvy street' to don the rough fabric of armed service uniforms. Everyone did what they could for King and Country and patriotism cut across social and religious boundaries. This was a war with a special meaning for the Jewish community but it was also a war for the survival of their adopted country. To fight under the British flag was an unquestioned duty.

Hardy/Goodman/Abdela/Moss

Keeping the Ultimate Anti-Semite at Bay

Hitler was the ultimate enemy of Jews and had to be kept at bay at all costs. If any of the British community needed to be persuaded to join up, this would be the message. At the beginning of the war, perhaps no-one could anticipate the lengths the Führer would go to in pursuit of his hatred of Jews, but the omens during the 1930s were already grim enough. It was time, once again, to visit the nearest recruitment office and to take up arms.

As already mentioned, a few of my relatives were to fight in both world wars, while in other cases it was the sons who followed in the footsteps of their fathers –

like Simon duParc Abraham's offspring, Julian and Donald. The elder of the two, Julian (Julian Du Parc Braham), was an avowed patriot who later campaigned for the restoration of monarchies in Europe. During the war, he served as an officer in the Royal Welsh Fusiliers. His brother, Donald, was also an officer and served as such until the war ended in 1945.

Jacob Abdela (later to be known as 'Judge Jack') was another officer who served for the duration of the war, prior to a distinguished career in the courts. Nor was he the only 'celebrity' in my extended family to play his part in the conflict, as the photographer, Baron, was a second lieutenant with the King's Shropshire Light Infantry.

My uncle, Jack Beilin (the husband of Josephine Hardy), sustained an injury to his back while serving in Dunkirk. The injury caused problems for the rest of his life but he refused to let it stop him from doing what he wanted. I recall him walking briskly along the bank of the Thames near his home in Richmond, with his two spaniels running ahead, using his stick only to keep them on the path.

Aunt Lottie (her real name being Jennie), a sister of my paternal grandfather, married a man called Philip Rodband Turner. During the war they went to live in Devon with their three children, one of whom was Harold Arthur, who worked as a librarian. Because of his age, he was conscripted and chose to join the RAF (23 Squadron), where he trained as a pilot. The expected lifespan of a pilot was short and Harold's aircraft was shot down in March 1944 over the Mediterranean. He was duly buried in Malta, the nearest British stronghold.

When, for one reason or another, the men were not conscripted (usually on account of age), they would volunteer for other duties. My cousin, Lesley Abdela, tells me how this was the case with her father, Fred:

> *He was aged over 30 when WW2 began. This was considered too old for the draft so during the war he volunteered for the London Fire Service at Battersea Fire Station, on the river fire-boat Massey Shaw, fire-fighting during the blitz. He then joined the Royal Naval Reserve – I still have his white naval roll-neck oiled wool sweater. I recall my father talking about the sound of the depth charges being dropped overboard to deter submarines when he sailed across the Atlantic for the first time, in March 1945. I also recall him mentioning Nova Scotia, so possibly they disembarked there.*

Another close relative who did what he could on the home front was Harold Sagar, husband of Ida, another of the Hardy sisters. They have now both passed away but their son, David, confirms that his father was in the National Fire Service and served through the blitz in London. As he recalls:

I remember him coming home in the morning absolutely black with soot and smoke.

I can find only one example of a woman in our family joining up and that was Trixie, the youngest of the Hardy sisters. A photo shows her in WAAF uniform, with a man who is believed to be her husband, Frank Lake.

Wars, at any time, are traumatic events and no-one returns from the battlefield the same as they were before. The scars live on and some of the participants remain in need of support, physical or mental, for the rest of their lives.

This is acknowledged by an organization, the Association of Jewish Ex-Servicemen and Women (AJEX), dedicated to provide just this. It emerged from disparate remembrance groups after the First World War, when Jewish forces in Britain and the Commonwealth numbered some 50,000; this figure increased in the Second World War to 70,000 in the British armed forces alone. When there has been a just cause, Jews have never been reluctant to serve and, in my own experience, I have never come across any of my relatives who have done anything other than fly the flag of their adopted country.

Goodman

Standing up for England

Simon duParc Abrahams (known as Symie) is mentioned above, in the roll call of the First World War. The injury he sustained meant that, for the rest of his life, he invariably used a stick. I also remember that he had a very loud voice and it took me a while to learn that he wasn't always angry.

With my parents, we sometimes called in for tea and I recall some of the conversations that took place. On one occasion, Symie recounted a recent trip that he and Trixie had made to the local cinema. It used to be the practice that at the end of the performance the audience stood dutifully while the national anthem was played. No-one was expected to leave and, in the aftermath of war, feelings of patriotism ran high:

> *'But I saw this young man,' shouted Symie, 'he was still slouching in his seat. So I took my stick and tapped him quite firmly on his shoulder, reminding him to do his duty. He gave me a surly expression but at least he got to his feet.'*

For some reason, I always remember this story, which even as a young boy told me what it meant to be patriotic. I very much doubt one would see that kind of intervention now.

Being a Part of England

British Jewry since World War II provides a peculiarly striking example of a downward spiral of deaths exceeding births.[101]

There was never an edict that required Jews to assimilate into modern English society; that was hardly needed, nor would it have worked. Rabbis, in their Sabbath gatherings, did not instruct their congregations to do so. If anything, a contrary message was issued, at least in Orthodox communities, to the effect that everything should be done to adhere to their own traditions and maintain a strong Jewish identity. At the very least, those in favour of assimilation would have been well-advised to be wary. Reference could be made to the experience of Jews in Spain and Portugal, all those years ago, for whom the only choice was either to convert to Christianity or leave the country. And if they did choose to convert, where did that get them? Closer to present times, the same argument could be applied to the integration of Jews in modern Germany, where they contributed to the professions and arts as well as business, and yet were murdered, simply because they were not of Aryan stock. Better, was the message, to live together and marry your own kind; we can be courteous to our neighbours, and law-abiding, but why go beyond that? To start with, this advice was heeded but, over time, it seemed that the outwardly solid structure of Jewish society was left on shaky foundations. Assimilation became the order of the day, and, as we will see, there were undoubted benefits but also costs.

The Right Address

Living together has very different connotations in Jewish history. It can mean being herded together under duress, forced into designated compounds; it can mean living together in a close-knit community with other Jews, by choice, as free individuals; or it can mean living without boundaries, in neighbourhoods combining Jews and gentiles alike.

Into the Ghetto

At different times during the diaspora, Jews were forced to live in specified areas, often surrounded by a wall and guarded to restrict access. This kind of containment preceded the introduction of a term to describe it, but from the early seventeenth century the Venetian practice of separating its Jewish residents in this way gave birth to the generic word, 'ghetto'. The reason for the term was clear enough: Ghetto was the name of an island in the lagoon, where the Jewish population was, effectively, corralled. They were confined to this one island and Christian watchmen guarded the gates to ensure that the rest of the city remained out of bounds. It is, at the very least, a humiliating concept, removing rightful freedoms and treating Jews as second-class citizens to be kept apart from the rest of the population.

But in the Second World War it became more than that, exemplified most fully by the example of the Warsaw Ghetto. Of all the ghettos created by the Nazis, this was by far the largest. The initial population of 350,000 grew with the arrival of refugees to a total of 450,000. A wall was built by the forced labour of the inhabitants themselves and, although the Jewish community comprised 30% of Warsaw's population at the start of the war, the wall contained just 2.4% of the city's area. The population within the walls bore no relationship to previous densities and conditions were desperately cramped and unhealthy; an estimated 80,000 died through hunger and disease, although that might have been a small mercy as the survivors were soon to be transported by train to Treblinka for mass extermination. Few managed to escape the ghetto, although one survivor could reflect:

> *At least we could break out of the ghetto, or at least die honourably, not as a stain on the face of history.*[102]

Because of its fearful associations, one might have thought that the word 'ghetto' would have disappeared from use with the end of the war, but it lives on in a generic sense as a disadvantaged part of any city, usually the home of a particular ethnic group. There might no longer be a wall to define the modern ghetto, but for the impoverished who live in these areas and cannot move to a better part of the city there might just as well be.

Living Together

In contrast, for Jews who can exercise their own free will, and choose to live close together in their own community, the experience is totally different. Time and again, Jews have elected to do this. Living in close contact with each other has been a source of strength throughout the Jewish diaspora. As well as offering a sense of security in an alien environment, it has other advantages, not least of all so that families and friends could provide help and support when needed. Many of the services and facilities they would look for, like a communal room for prayer or a ritual slaughter yard, would be accessible. Networks are especially important for immigrants, who by their very nature are unfamiliar with their new surroundings and are often in need of help and reassurance. This sense of 'togetherness' can easily be interpreted as being exclusive but it has been more a question of survival.

That all sounds very functional but one can turn again to Israel Zingwall for a reminder that there is more to it than that. Even (or perhaps especially) in times of hardship, Jewish communities have shown themselves to be places of enormous vitality, resilience and a natural predisposition to help each other. We have already seen instances where Zangwill drew on his experience of London's East End around the turn of the nineteenth and twentieth centuries, to describe what he saw. Hemmed in by crowded tenements and workshops, it was a noisy place, with the clatter of machines, the hammering of wood and, most of all, the foreign-sounding voices. Yiddish remained for a time the common language although words were gradually Anglicized to produce a unique hybrid that could just about be understood by outsiders. Everyone worked long hours with little prospect of achieving much more than they needed to live on, although, even in those circumstances, humour was never far away. People would laugh, especially when someone acted above their station, speaking as if their tiny workshop was the centre of the business world. And they laughed (not without sympathy) at the hapless Moses Ansell, one of life's eternal losers:

> ... *whose versatility was marvellous. There was nothing he could not do badly. He had been glazier, synagogue beadle, picture-frame manufacturer, cantor, peddler, shoemaker in all branches, coat-seller, official executioner of fowls and cattle, Hebrew teacher, fruiterer, circumciser, professional corpse-watcher, and now he was a tailor out of work.* [103]

Living Apart

As confidence grew, and other opportunities presented themselves, the question was asked: why should I continue to live near my parents and everyone else I grew up with? It was time to branch out, breaking free from the invisible ties of Jewishness. Especially if the synagogue was no longer the centre of the local universe, and it was no longer essential to rely on kosher food stores, one could live anywhere.

A new generation chose to do just that, following the advice of estate agents rather than rabbis. Young men and women, making their way in the world, didn't want to do what was expected of them. They wanted to break free. An increasing number were 'marrying out' and were drawn by their partner's wishes as well as their own. But there was another reason, too, for dispersal. As I know from my own experience, not everyone wants to be branded as Jewish. That is not a question of rejection so much as saying that it is time to be one's own person. I chose to go to a university that was far from any Jewish community, and to do anything but live in Golders Green. In time, serendipity played its part, and in due course my wife and I were washed up on the shores of Seychelles. As far as I can tell, there is only one other Jew on the island and, as chance would have it, he lives on the neighbouring plot. Serendipity again.

Marrying Out

For generations, Jews lived in closed communities, where it was unusual, if not a sin, to do anything but marry within your religion. In time, though, marrying out was to become ever more common. How did this happen? The answer is that young Jewish men and women were no longer confined to the kind of self-imposed ghetto, shaped by tradition, that defined all of their activities. There was a world beyond the Jewish community and new opportunities to meet young people of other faiths. Students at university, professionals in their place of work, and a selection of holidays that offered more than Jewish summer camps. The word of parents was no longer law and rabbis lost the authority they once enjoyed. In any case, in the postwar period, especially from the 1960s, things were changing for all young people. Structures that previously held society together were becoming less rigid. Tradition gave way to modernity, religious doctrine to free will.

Of all the changes that have taken place in the Jewish world, marrying out is probably the one with the greatest impact. The world has changed and long gone is the day when a Jewish history could be limited to a traditional marriage within the faith, assuring its people of continuity. Social change and assimilation have rewritten the terms of engagement and this opens up different questions and answers.

Currently, in roughly a quarter of all 'Jewish' marriages in Britain, one of the partners is not Jewish; the proportion of non-Jewish partners is higher where couples cohabit. The figure is even higher in my own family. I have been married twice, both times out of my religion; my brother did the same in his first marriage, although his second wife's father was Jewish; and my sister also chose to marry out of the faith. What is more telling is that the children of the generation that succeeds mine have also married out. Elsewhere amongst my relatives, there have been instances of both – marrying in and marrying out – but in most cases the next generation has opted for the latter.

In stark terms, every time a man chooses a gentile for his wife, the family is lost to the Jewish faith. Or at least it is statistically. Certainly, the facts are compelling. In the immediate postwar period the number of Jews in Britain was in the region of 420,000; it fell to about 260,000 at the beginning of this century and has risen slightly since then.[104] Within this range, there are significant differences, depending on the proportion of

Orthodox Jews in an area; where there is a high concentration, there will be large families and little or no marrying out. Thus:

> *Those areas of the country with large concentrations of strictly Orthodox Jews (Stamford Hill, north-west London, north Manchester and Gateshead) all saw significant increases, whilst areas associated with mainstream Jewry, such as Redbridge and Brent [both in London] saw declining Jewish populations.*[105]

But statistics are not everything and, in a sensitive treatment of the subject, Emma Klein questions the age-old rule of matrilineal descent to determine Jewish identity.[106] Rabbis came to that conclusion in the earliest days of the Jewish religion. But there is no inherent reason, she suggests, why the father of a family cannot be equally important in matters of religion, especially if the children are brought up to understand and practice Jewish doctrine and to celebrate the main festivals. Klein has interviewed a large number of rabbis and members of mixed families alike and the results lend support for her questioning of convention. She concludes that marrying out can be a source of religious strength rather than weakness, citing the view of one of her interviewees that if you want to be Jewish, then be Jewish, whatever that means for you. In any case, it is not unusual to find some partners in a mixed marriage converting to the Jewish religion. We should be looking for ways to recover what Klein terms the 'lost Jews' rather than abandon them because of a questionable restriction.

It is sad that people feel compelled to make a choice; it should not be a question of 'either/or'. Assimilation can offer the best of both worlds, being a Jew and being British. In a multi-racial society there is no need to turn one's back on one or the other. Orthodox Jews have every right to live within their own community and practice their own beliefs but they should not seek to impose that choice on others. Jews have more freedom now than at any time in history, to assimilate or not, to emigrate to the Promised Land or not. This is surely what has been sought, but never before enjoyed, over so many years. The crumbling of ghetto walls should be celebrated not mourned.

Chapter 8

Shakespeare's Folly

More than four centuries after the Bard of Avon rested his quill, having completed yet another of his enduring works, the imagery of The *Merchant of Venice* remans as sharp as ever. One only has to mention the title of the play for the figure of Shylock, the Jewish moneylender, to be brought to mind in all his exaggerated details. Shakespeare spared nothing in portraying this central character in the way that everyone expected and no-one would forget.

The fact is that the portrayal had little to do with history and more with the kind of stereotyping that followed Jews around. It was unlikely that anyone in England at that time had even met a Jew, as they were all expelled from the country at the end of the thirteenth century. And even before that, in the period when they had been allowed to settle, numbers were relatively small and they were rarely seen in most parts of the country. But Shakespeare knew there was enough ill feeling to give meaning to his treatment of Shylock, the uncompromising moneylender in Venice.

Shylock was already despised in the trading community of his city because of the hard terms he exacted to lend money; so when his bitter adversary, Antonio, approached him for a loan on behalf of a friend, Bassanio, it was no time to soften his approach. The sum in question was not great, but Shylock insisted that if it was not repaid on time Antonio would have to concede a pound of his own flesh. Through no fault of his own, Antonio defaulted and Shylock demanded his rightful due, in effect, condemning the hapless borrower to almost certain death. Suffice to say that Shylock was caricatured as grasping and totally mercenary, without a care for anything or anyone else. Successive actors of note – including Dustin Hoffman, Warren Mitchell and Al Pacino – have played the part to the full, depicting Shylock as hook-nosed and bearded, guileful and miserly, with a foreign accent and suspicion of gentiles, in short, in every way a Jewish stereotype to be reviled.

If it were a pantomime production, the audience would boo at his very appearance on stage, but this is Shakespeare and while at times Shylock is, indeed, the devil incarnate, at other times he attracts sympathy and understanding. Speaking, as it were, for all Jews who are vilified, it comes almost as a shock that he can then invite remorse, reminding his accusers that he is a human being just as they are:

I am a Jew. Hath not a Jew eyes? Hath not a Jew hands, organs, dimensions, senses, affections, passions; fed with the same food, hurt with the same weapons, subject to the same diseases, healed by the same means, warmed and cooled by the same winter and summer as a Christian is? If you prick us, do we not bleed?[107]

It is this subtle change of pace that explains why even Jewish actors have lined up to play this contentious role. And it is this which removes it from the firing line of outright anti-Semitism, calling for reflection rather than rebuke. In the present, febrile atmosphere of political correctness it is questionable whether a contemporary playwright would get such a work accepted. It can easily be used in anti-Semitic rhetoric but there is more to it than that. Shylock's daughter causes her father consternation by 'marrying out', something the Jewish caricature that was Shylock could never have contemplated nor come to terms with. Life is complex and, perhaps, what could easily be misconstrued as Shakespeare's folly can, on reflection, invite a more nuanced response. Down the years, Shylock has remained a 'hate' figure for those who want to see it that way but, Shakespeare's portrayal reveals a multitude of emotions and motives.

Circumstances vary but the very presence of anti-Semitism is unremittingly evil. Most telling is that, in one form or another, it never goes away. Even today, there cannot be a Jew who has not personally experienced an aspect of anti-Semitism, however mildly, myself being no exception. It has become part of Jewish history, to be borne but also overcome.

'Some Were Neighbours'

Some were workers, some teachers, some neighbours. Many ordinary people enabled the Holocaust simply by doing their jobs. Some made the choice to help, while others decided to join in with the persecution, betraying Jewish friends and classmates.[108]

Anti-Semitism, which has hounded Jews throughout most of their history, is expressed in different ways. At one extreme is the unparalleled example of the Nazi Holocaust, resulting in the murder of millions. The sheer numbers, combined with meticulous planning, make this horrendous event different in kind from anything else, although in many ways it was simply the culmination of a succession of massacres and persecution with a long pedigree. Jew-baiting was nothing new by the time that Hitler came to power, whether the outcome was to add to the tally of deaths or expulsion from a nation to rid the hosts of their presence.

As the opening quote in this section suggests, quite apart from out-and-out Jew-haters, more moderate sections of society can be brought into the arena too. It is to England's credit that, year on year, this kind of readiness to respond to extremism has been slowly outlawed so that most people would now consider such views unacceptable. This has been a gradual process but progress can be measured by the kind of language that was admissible at the time that parliament was debating whether restrictions should be lifted to allow all Jews to have access to the same rights as given to Christians. There were then no restraints on what people could say, and in one of the many debates in the British House of Commons in the nineteenth century, on removing the restrictions which debarred Jews from various professional and public offices, some members used it as an opportunity to say what they really thought. William Cobbett, the member of parliament for the Lancashire town of Oldham (who championed traditional values but is sometimes considered a radical in other respects) spoke his mind in no uncertain terms. As a rival speaker reported:

> *The honorable member for Oldham tells us that the Jews are naturally a mean race, a sordid race, a money-getting race; that they are averse to all honorable callings; that they neither sow nor reap; that they have neither flocks nor herds; that usury is the only pursuit for which they are fit; that they are destitute of all elevated and amiable sentiments. Such has in every age been the reasoning of bigots.*[109]

Cobbett's views could well have incited a violent reaction against Jews, of a sort that was seen elsewhere in Europe. But, fortunately, there were opposing voices, in favour of emancipation, and good sense prevailed.

Although England in the modern era has repeatedly veered away from extremism, anti-Semitism never completely goes away. It simply reappears in different forms. Sometimes these are subtle manifestations like playground taunts, snubbing and asides by neighbours. But, although there have been repeated instances of anti-Semitism, Jews in this country have generally benefited from a sense of fairness in British society, which has kept it within bounds. Rational argument would be listened to and would sometimes win the day. As far back as 1911, my great-uncle, Meyer Dubowski, for instance, was so incensed by the bigotry that lost him a dairy supply contract, that his protest came to the attention of *The Jewish Chronicle*.

Moss

'No Milk Today'

Under the heading, 'Bethnal Green: An Admirable Rebuke', the report (published in 1911) reads:

A word of appreciation is due to the Great Eastern Dairy Co., for the dignified manner in which it has refused to take up the milk contract that the Bethnal Green Guardians recently conceded after a first refusal on the ground of race or religion. The proprietor of the firm (Mr S.M. Dubowski) reminds the Guardians of the "disgraceful and bigoted method" in which his tender was originally dealt with, and informs them that the Guardians "having imported into this discussion the question of religion", he feels that he would be discrediting his firm and his own integrity, if he allowed "this very grave matter" to pass as though nothing had happened. This is excellently said and we do not envy the feelings of the better men on the Bethnal Green Board when they read this richly-merited rebuke. It is satisfactory to see that the folly of those Guardians has not been initiated elsewhere – a fact which indicates that racial or religious bigotry in this country is confined within very narrow limits – so far, at all events, as municipal bodies go. For the rest, Mr Dubowski's action will teach the valuable lesson that there are two things which Jews – keen business men though they be – hold above mercantile gain: racial honour and personal self-respect. The contrast thus exhibited with the prime movers in the recent incident may well be left to the public judgement.

I am proud of my Uncle Meyer, who took on his grievance single-handed. Things, however, in the same part of London, took an altogether uglier turn in the 1930s, requiring a different kind of response. Taking their lead from the growing violence in Germany during that period, the British Fascist movement, led by Oswald Mosley, looked to fan the flames in England in a similar way. This came to a head in 1936, when Mosley's black-shirted followers planned a march through the heart of the Jewish community in the East End. In what was known as the Battle of Cable Street, the intruders were duly rebutted, not only by the Jews themselves but also by a large contingent of Irish and other anti-Fascist groups.[110] Unlike their counterparts in Hitler's Germany, the Jews of east London were not alone. Moreover, Fascism in this country never gained the ascendancy that it did on the European mainland. Little wonder when the time came to join the fight against the Nazis, Jews from this and other parts of Britain were not slow to sign up.

One of the quirks of history is that, in spite of all that happened in the war against the Nazis and their allies, the immediate postwar period did not see the end of anti-Semitism. It was evident in this country but, perhaps, even more starkly in the United States where it seemed that people could still say and do what they wished. American country clubs in the early and mid-twentieth century offer an array of examples of ways to stop Jews joining an essentially white, Protestant community, ranging from the excuse that the club was full (when it was not) to outright rejection. It is only fifty years since the Baltimore Country Club, for instance, could brazenly display a notice reading 'No Dogs, No Coloreds, No Jews'.[111] Prejudice may still linger behind the scenes but, in all democracies, there is at last a taboo on giving needless offence to minorities.

To Leave or Not to Leave

The risk of a wrong decision is preferable to terror of indecision.[112]

Jews have so often been unwelcome, wherever they went; but one cannot make the assumption that they were always forced to move from one place to another. They may well have decided to move for other reasons; because they thought they could make a better living elsewhere, for example. Indeed, the hardest question in this narrative is to ask exactly *why* my various ancestors repeatedly made the decision to leave where they were (and where their family might have lived for generations before). And I must ask, too, why so many family members eventually chose to come and live in England. Unfortunately, there was no fly on the wall to listen to those conversations round the kitchen table, about the rights and wrongs of uprooting and moving to a new land about which they knew so little. And, of course, the present generation of family members has missed the chance to ask such questions of them personally. So whether it was a case of gathering a few belongings and leaving without delay, or the result of a long-thought-out plan; sadly, there is little in the way of old letters or other documents to tell us more.

There is an obvious gap in the records but I am loath to simply leave a gap in the text. The fact is that we do know some things, albeit generic. We know of specific events that might have encouraged people to leave when they did. And we have good records about the pattern of immigration in England, including where the newcomers came from. We also know how Jews fared in their new country of adoption, concentrating first on getting a foothold and then, themselves and through future generations, making their own contribution to society. In other words, even if details about individuals are missing, we know a lot about general trends. This can usefully provide a framework for individual accounts. But it is all background information – circumstantial evidence – and one must ask whether this is enough to describe why various family members moved to England? As any historian will confirm, the answer has to be 'no'. An essential piece in the puzzle is missing and cannot be recreated as it was.

Such is the reality of this particular line of historical research. Yet, using what facts are known, I believe there is a way to at least offer a partial representation of what happened. In all of the other chapters, the various cameos are based directly on the experience of real people and actual records. In this section, because of the hole in the data, I would like to do something different, openly mixing facts with fiction. Thus, in the four cameos that follow, the characters are fictional (although loosely based on what is known about actual ancestors), while the circumstances they faced are rooted in fact. I know where my relatives came from, and when each made the move to England. With the indulgence of readers, I would like to speculate *why* they did this.

Four stories have been written, each illustrating a different journey. The first traces the migration from Hanover of a well-established family, in many ways model citizens in German society; the second follows an unusual route, from the New World and back to the Old; the third starts by the warm waters of the Mediterranean before a carefully-considered move to Manchester; while the final cameo tells of a journey from the Pale of western Russia to the East End of London. Our families do, indeed, come from far and wide and there is more than a grain of truth in each of these compilations. But I have also allowed fiction to fill in the gaps and to create an impressionistic rather than a strictly genealogical account. The one thing they all have in common is that, in different ways, they escaped the perennial threat of anti-Semitism.

Leaving Hanover

Harpsichord Discord

The name of Simon Finkelstein was known and respected, not only in his home town of Hanover, in north Germany, but elsewhere in the region. He was an unassuming man but it was not his character that gave him his reputation. It was, instead, because he made the most perfect harpsichords; and middle-class families wanted nothing more than to own one, embossed in gold with the distinctive 'Finkelstein' signature so that all would know where it came from.

Harpsichords are enormously complex to make, calling for technical excellence to convert a touch of the keyboard into a plucking motion that produces a sound that immediately evokes thoughts of baroque. No less challenging is the casing for the instrument, calling for a different set of skills, and which itself has to be a work of art. Simon learned his multi-faceted craft from an early age and through his own flair coupled with a propensity to work all hours to achieve perfection, he built a successful business.

On the surface, his life was as harmonious as the music that came from his instruments. He was Jewish but not especially religious, never missing the festivals but not always seen at shul on the sabbath. His marriage to a Jewish wife, Sarah, was all that he could wish for and, knowing of her husband's commitment to his business, she devoted much of her own time to their three children and to voluntary work in the community.

There were many other Jews in Hanover in the late-nineteenth century (some 4000 in total), so the Finkelsteins were never short of friends and family members nearby.

(...cont'd)

And, for business reasons as well as to show respect for his country, both Simon and Sarah spoke German and kept abreast of current affairs. All was well, but Simon had a music maker's ear for a wrong note and something was not quite as it should be. Germany, like other European countries, had its own, long history of anti-Semitism and at times different Jewish communities had been persecuted and even expelled. But in his own time, in the nineteenth century, emancipation measures had been passed into law. Most of his customers were gentiles, and relations were always polite. And yet, the barely discernible sound of a note that was so very slightly off-key was enough to keep him awake at night.

For all his attempts to embrace and be a part of German society he knew that he would never be fully accepted. Beneath the surface there were too many people who, to put it mildly, disliked Jews. That in itself might have been bearable – and clearly it was, amongst most of his Jewish friends – but what was to stop this simmering dislike becoming something more? What was to stop it boiling over into violence, just as had been evident in the past? Simon read and listened to what was happening in other parts of Europe, especially in Russian territory to the east, and it sent a chill down his spine. 'I can see a cloud', he thought, 'but one day that will turn into a storm'.

Sarah was more sanguine about the prospects but, loyal to her husband, she understood his view. When Simon's concerns turned to thoughts about leaving the country where they were both born it seemed that there was little to stop them. They had put to one side some useful savings and Simon had already been thinking of selling the business and leading an easier life. With his outstanding skills and reputation for the quality of his work, he would never be out of a job if he wanted it. Both their parents had passed away and they would not be leaving behind any other dependants. Their children were all in their early twenties and largely without ties. None of them had yet married.

It was the first decade of the new century and they were aware of how many Jews were making the same decision, leaving continental Europe in droves for a new life elsewhere. The United States was the favoured destination but the Finkelsteins both felt more comfortable with the thought of England. With its established conventions and no recent history of violence, Simon saw that it could offer a more secure environment for all of the family.

Through his business contacts he knew which parts of London would be suitable. He wanted to avoid the East End, which offered a refuge for the poorest in the community and he chose, instead, a new suburb in the north-west of the capital.

The journey to England was simple enough and on a warm summer's day in 1906 they took a train to Hamburg, where they embarked on a ship for the voyage across the North Sea.

It was the right decision and very far-sighted. Being model German citizens would not have spared them from what was to happen, when being Jewish was all that counted. Thirty years passed before the violence that Simon had anticipated really came to the boil. Even before a national boycott of Jewish businesses in 1933, Hanover saw its own anti-Jewish riots and the dismissal by the main department store in the city of all of its Jewish staff. Year by year the situation worsened:

> *Jews understood their perilous plight; many left and others closed their business and professional practices. By 1938, 552 Jewish business and legal and medical practices in Hanover were no longer operating. As their public life as Germans narrowed, Jewish communal life became more intense... On Kristalnacht the synagogue was burned, Jewish stores were looted and homes ransacked. The mortuary was also destroyed and the mikveh was wrecked.*[113]

The deportations from Hanover started soon after, and by 1945 there were very few left of what was once a flourishing community. With the ending of the war, just 66 survivors returned to the city, less to start new lives than to mourn what had been lost.[114]

Was it more by luck than judgement that so many Jewish families made the right decision in leaving their homes in continental Europe? Hanover was in the firing line but, as we will see, so were other places where my relatives had lived. Had the Finkelsteins remained, it is probable that they would all have ended their lives in a concentration camp. Somehow, whether by accident or design, they all avoided that terrible plight, and thank God for that.

Leaving Montreal

Montreal *Adieu*

The story of Freda Weitzman is unusual in that it takes her, against the general trend of migration, from the New World back to Europe. She was born in Montreal, Canada in 1875, into a well-to-do household. Her family had been settled in Montreal for two generations, having left their previous home in Amsterdam early in the nineteenth century, following the end of the Napoleonic Wars.

Before arriving in Amsterdam, the Weitzman family had made their way in stages, over more than three centuries, from Spain, where they were expelled with all other Jews in 1492. Like many of their fellow refugees, they went first to France, to Provence and then Alsace, moving on when local opposition to Jews gave their latest predicament a sense of urgency. Holland, they were told, offered a more tolerant setting, so that is where they headed. In fact, not all of Holland was welcoming to Jews, the conservative attitudes of traditional Protestants finding it difficult to deal with outsiders espousing a different religion. But Amsterdam was special, offering not only a sanctuary but also numerous business opportunities. The liberal, enterprising environment of a city that was renowned for its international connections suited Freda's great-grandfather, Benjamin, who soon became a succesful shipping merchant. In spite of this, he was a restless soul by nature and was easily lured by distant horizons and the prospect of new opportunities. Perhaps it was bound to happen that, as he looked out to sea, and spoke to sea captains, one day he would succumb to temptation; so much so that early in the nineteenth century he booked a passage for his family on a ship bound for Canada.

From what he had heard, Montreal was the place to be, a gateway port for the vast hinterland that had yet to be exploited. The fact that most people at the time spoke French in Montreal was not a deterrent, and he and his family soon made themselves at home in the new milieu. It was only natural that he should continue in shipping and international trade, a wise decision in terms of its profitability. Benjamin's son joined his father in the business, which continued to prosper and, in turn, his grandson, Solomon (Freda's father) followed suit.

In due course, there was a lively debate about which city would be chosen as Canada's capital. Montreal and Toronto were the front-runners and Solomon invested heavily in land in Montreal that he thought could later be sold for government buildings. In the event, in 1867, Ottawa was selected and Benjamin had to be content with recouping his investments, more or less at cost. Although he did not incur serious losses, his confidence was dented and he felt that he had lost face in the close-knit community (by then there were some 400 Jews in Montreal) where he was well-known. Solomon, like his ancestors, was impetuous and decided that he and his family should leave 'provincial' Montreal and move back to Europe, this time to the world's trading capital, London.

Freda was only five when they arrived in England, living at first in a large house in west London. With the help of his many existing contacts, her father's business fared even better than before. London was at the heart of an empire and world trade seemed to have no limits.

With this kind of financial security, Freda grew up in comfortable surroundings and would often be brought, with her brothers and sisters, to meet some of the business acquaintances who were invited to the house. Sometimes she was invited to play the piano for the guests. When her schooling finished, she did what was expected of her as a young lady. The actions and cause of suffragettes, who were demonstrating in central London at the time, attracted no interest in her. But the thought of marriage did, and there was one visitor she had within her sights.

David Levi was a Sephardi Jew who lived and worked mainly in Manchester. He came to London on a regular basis and it was noticed that his visits to west London became more frequent. When he asked Freda for her hand in marriage, there was no hesitation, and the vow was sealed. Freda duly moved to Manchester with her husband. She was used to living in a large house with servants and David ensured that high standards would continue. Unfortunately, his business later suffered setbacks and took its toll on his health. When he died, in 1930, Freda had to leave the big house and move to an apartment, first in London and, when the war came, in Brighton.

On a crackly wireless, she listened every day to reports of allied forces fighting the Nazis. It was clear that things were not going well for Jews on the continent, and there were rumours of mass evacuations from the cities where most had lived. But it was only when the war ended that the truth about concentration camps was revealed. Freda wept when she heard the stories. She wept out of sheer relief that she and her family had been spared, and she wept for the millions of her own people who had been murdered. She knew that it was by chance that she had come to England, and (although not a religious woman) she prayed nightly to give thanks for her salvation.

Leaving Aleppo

Pomegranates and Palatine Road

Samuel Betesh was born in Aleppo and it was there that he later set up a trading company, specializing in buying and selling cotton that was grown in the irrigated fields of Egypt and Iraq. In the course of his business he travelled widely in the region and at times he also made the journey to Manchester, where he became familiar with the world's largest concentration of spinning and weaving mills. One of his early trips was to the coastal town of Arta in western Greece, which he used as a base to explore the potential of a growing market for cotton. While in Arta he met leading members of an established Sephardi community, and amongst them the woman, Lydia, who was to be his future wife.

After their marriage, a joyous occasion that brought together the whole of the Sephardi community in Arta, the couple settled in Samuel's hometown. Samuel loved Aleppo and could never imagine living anywhere else. They owned a small but comfortable house with a courtyard and, when Lydia gave birth to three sons and two daughters, Samuel liked nothing better than to sit in the shade of a pomegranate tree, sipping fresh lemonade, and watching them play. The pace and quality of Levantine life suited him well.

When people speak of the Jewish diaspora it is often thought that this refers to the journeys made westwards across the Mediterranean, and northwards into eastern and central Europe. Yet many Jews stayed close to Palestine, finding refuge in the surrounding countries, like Iraq, Egypt and Syria. They had much in common with the Arab majority and, as part of the Ottoman Empire, there were generally no problems. It was a large region but networks were formed and visitors from Egypt and Iraq were not unusual. Sometimes this led to the marriage of a boy or girl in Aleppo with a Jewish counterpart from one of the neighbouring countries, a Shasha or Nahum, a Sassoon or Hassan, producing an exotic Levantine mix.

Samuel travelled widely but he would always try to include one or two trips each year to Arta, home of Lydia's relatives, and the nearby island of Corfu. The Jewish communities were well established and he felt very much at home. On one of these occasions he was surprised to hear talk amongst some of the people he met, of leaving the region in favour of settling in Manchester.

He had visited Manchester himself and, fascinating though it was, it was also cold, wet and smoky. Why, he asked, would anyone wish to make a permanent move to such a place? The answer he was given offered him food for thought. Both Corfu and Arta were amenable places to live, they would say, but the population was small and business opportunities limited. What will our children do when they grow up? To add to that, there were political complications. In the case of Corfu, the security provided by the British to the people of Corfu had recently ended, when the island was ceded to newly-independent Greece. Arta was an even stranger case, having been excluded at the time of its formation from Greece (and only transferred later in the century). Would Greece always be so tolerant of the Jews in its country, and would the ousted Ottomans one day try to restore the territory they had lost in the Greek War of Independence?

On the journey back to Aleppo these things he had never thought of before now occupied his mind. It is true, he thought, that Jews are always dependent on the whims of the host country and a situation can change overnight. Samuel himself had heard murmurings of Arab opposition to Jewish purchases of land in Palestine, although he had not previously connected this with his family's own welfare. When he next went to Manchester, he vowed to find out more about the possibilities. He took with him the names of business contacts provided by his Arta and Corfu friends and he wasted no time in meeting people and also seeing where fellow merchants and their families lived. Given the history of the diaspora it was hardly surprising that people like Samuel would be wary.

On his return to Aleppo, he and Lydia talked it through. There was no immediate reason to leave their much-loved home but it might not always be so secure, especially if Arab nationalism continued to gather pace. Manchester undoubtedly offered better business opportunities and, when their children grew up, there were many different things they could do. By comparison, much though they found it difficult to imagine being anywhere else, Aleppo was provincial in comparison with the home of King Cotton. The way forward, they agreed, was for Samuel to take lodgings on his next visit and explore more fully how he could relocate his business and then to see whether they should make the move. It helped that some of his Greek friends and relatives had already done so, and he visited one family in a large house in what was called Palatine Road. There were other Sephardi Jews in the district and a new synagogue had been built to serve their needs. The Betesh family would certainly not be alone.

Samuel's business was successful and he could afford to buy a large house, of the sort he had seen on his most recent visit. So the die was cast, and he and his family were soon to make their own arrangements to move. In due course, they spent time in the gardens and drawing rooms of neighbours and friends who had previously known the warm winds of the Levant and they would often reminisce. But they never regretted the move, which had opened up all kinds of opportunity, and when they were formally naturalized they slipped easily into the status of being British. Their children even more so.

Leaving Minsk

The Kippahs of Minsk

Daniel and Miriam Levitski, with their four young children, arrived in Whitechapel, bedraggled and exhausted, in the winter of 1887. It had been a long and arduous journey that saw them leave their former home in Minsk on a bitterly cold New Year's Day, destined for a new life in a land about which they knew little. They carried their few possessions with them and, with their modest savings, they bought food along the way and then tickets for the sea voyage from Bremerhaven to the Port of London. Temperatures on the overland leg of the journey were well below freezing but the family was used to that and made light of the difficult conditions. While they waited a couple of days for the boat that would take them to London, they clustered in a crowded shed on the dockside with many other emigrants, all travelling west. Most, though, were booked for a transatlantic crossing to New York. The Levitskis had thought about that but were persuaded by Miriam's brother, Mordecai, to make their way to London. Mordecai had made the same journey a few years earlier and his knowledge of the city and contacts there seemed too valuable to turn down.

Miriam believed that her own ancestors, and probably those of Daniel too, had come originally to Minsk from Germany to escape constant threats to their lives. For several centuries, the eastern provinces of Europe had offered a more secure existence, and they got on with their lives as best they could. Daniel had learned from his father the skills of hat-making, specializing in those items of headwear which were part of religious ritual. He was known for the quality of his *kippahs* (more commonly known in Minsk as *yarmulke*) and also the distinctive fur hat, the *shtreimel*, worn mainly by Hasidic Jews. With a large Jewish community in the region he was assured of a steady demand for his products. It was also a trade in which Miriam could help, and she was always there to look after the workshop when Daniel went away at times to sell his hats in the surrounding towns and villages. They would never get rich but made just enough to feed and clothe their family and for Moses to attend *shul* on the sabbath, as well for them all to celebrate the Jewish holidays. Nearby were relatives, and friends they had made in the tight-knit community. If things had stayed as they were, it is unlikely that the Levitskis would have felt a need to move. But these were Jews of the diaspora, subject, as they had always been, to the changing fortunes of their host countries, which they were powerless to influence. Decisions would be made far away yet close enough to change forever their own circumstances. And that is precisely what happened in this case.

After centuries of tolerant rule under the Grand Duchy of Lithuania, and then the Polish-Lithuanian Commonwealth, in 1791 the territory was ceded to Russia. Jews were not favoured by the new rulers, who immediately introduced the Pale of Settlement, restricting where they could live. So long as they conformed, life would continue much as before, but the situation was far from stable. When, in 1881, Tsar Alexander II was assassinated, the Jews were automatically (and erroneously) blamed for the incident.

This accusation, in turn, triggered a series of pogroms, with the inevitable loss of life and destruction of property. The new Tsar, Alexander III, was known to hate Jews with a vengeance and things would only get worse. It made sense to leave Minsk, as thousands were already doing, but it still took time to be sure and to make arrangements for the elderly relatives who chose to stay behind. By the end of 1886, they were ready to leave and London would soon be the family's new home.

When they arrived in the Port of London they were given a warm welcome. Thanks to Miriam's brother, accommodation had already been found for the family and, as well as this, Daniel was offered a small corner of a nearby workshop so that he could resume the work he was familiar with without too much delay.

The children bore the sudden change well and quickly conversed in Yiddish with their new neighbours. But Miriam was insistent that they should all learn English, their new mother tongue. It was a wise move and helped the children to find work when they grew up.

None of them wanted to take on their father's business, preferring to seek jobs of their own choice. One of the sons, who was especially good at maths, became a teacher at the nearby Stepney Jewish School, and one of the daughters, who was also very numerate, found work locally as a book-keeper. The other son was fascinated by electricity and learned more about the subject at night school, while the other daughter enjoyed cooking and was much in demand to cater for local events.

And, from one generation to another, this is how the children of the diaspora first gained a foothold in their new society, prior to advancing in directions determined by their own abilities and ambition. They no longer lived within the confines of the ghetto; they were now to be citizens of the world. Their children and their children's children.

Déjà Vu

The last survivors and the last perpetrators are about to leave our world and the Holocaust is changing from being something that is living memory to being part of history.[115]

The above words (of the Chief Rabbi of Moscow) are simple but poignant. Like a mighty monument, fabricated in stone, the Holocaust in the immediate postwar years cast its own shadow over a subdued continent. The terrifying reality of systematically murdering nearly six million Jews silenced even those who had been actively anti-Semitic before that; regardless of whether their views had really changed, it was simply not acceptable to be outspoken on the subject. But silence is not forever and within a generation or two some of the old expressions of hate could, once again, be heard. Many of these were, as in earlier times, voices of ignorance but, even worse, some were spoken by supposed academics who denied that the Holocaust had ever happened. One way and another, anti-Semitism emerged from the darkness, where it had lain hidden for more than half a century, to stalk the land anew.

The start of a new millennium has seen the re-telling of an old story. Across Europe, it seems that nowhere is immune from a resurgence of anti-Jewish sentiment, which in a disturbing number of cases has resulted in the loss of life. If much of this new wave of anti-Semitism has stayed beneath the radar, there is no avoiding the impact of some high-profile events. In Paris, for instance, in 2015 four Jews were killed while shopping in a kosher food store; three years later, the anniversary of these killings was marked by an incident in which another kosher store was destroyed by fire. Also in Paris, two elderly women were murdered in separate circumstances, one of whom was a concentration camp survivor. These events make the headlines but every day it seems that Jews are taunted, buildings defaced and threats are commonplace. France, with the largest Jewish population in Europe, has been especially targeted, so much so that many Jews have chosen to emigrate to Israel.

Elsewhere on the continent, four Jews were shot by a jihadist in the Jewish museum in Brussels. Even Germany, where there have been great efforts to distance itself from the past, there has been an increase in anti-Semitic offences. In looking for causes for the return of an old enemy, one has to acknowledge that, two generations after the demise of the National

Socialists in Germany, young people today have no direct experience of events then. It would be comforting to claim that humans learn from the past, but there is no obvious evidence to support that. As the Chief Rabbi of Moscow reminds us, the Holocaust is fast slipping from direct experience into history, leaving something of a vacuum for a new generation of Jew-haters. Foremost amongst these are Islamic immigrants who have made their home in Europe but who espouse different sets of values, including, for some, a virulent brand of anti-Zionism. It is Islamists who have been responsible for most of the killings recorded above. Recent years have also seen a rise in the influence of far-right political parties, which have been quick to include anti-Semitic slogans in their propaganda. For instance, though small in number, even a seemingly liberal society like Sweden has seen more than its fair share of attacks on Jews, incited by its main far-right party.

Nor has the UK fared much better. Jewish schools, synagogues and cemeteries have all been targeted, their walls daubed with offensive messages and images of the long-despised swastika. Some of my own relatives, who live in areas with a large Jewish population, tell of the need to be constantly alert and to play their own part in protecting communal buildings. Each day, children arriving at Jewish schools wend their way around security fences, in the presence of burly guards posted at the gates to keep them safe. And this is the twenty-first century, when, one might have thought, such behaviour belongs to the past. Moreover, there is a fear across the community that things will only get worse. To make the point, no-one expected that the Labour Party (one of the two main political parties in Britain, alternating power with the Conservative Party), historically the guardian of liberal policies and the home of some distinguished Jewish politicians and many supporters, would itself become a source of anti-Semitism. But that is exactly what has happened.[116]

It has been a sorry and unexpected episode in the history of a political organization which has in the past done much to improve the welfare of its people. The start of this phase of anti-Jewish behaviour can be dated to the election in 2015 of Jeremy Corbyn as the party's leader. Espousing policies that were far to the left, warning signs were already evident with his record of embracing the leadership of both Hezbollah and Hamas, outspoken enemies of Israel. Corbyn remained unrepentant about his links with these organizations but what was to cause greater disquiet was the extent to which many members within the party shared his views and went further with comments and actions that were unmistakably anti-Semitic. As well as opposing Zionism and the modern state of Israel, individuals resorted to the age-old cry that Jews controlled the world's financial institutions and manipulated them in favour of their own interests. It was the kind of accusation heard in Germany in the 1930s. Although an appropriate response by the leadership was called for, none was forthcoming. At least one Jewish MP received death threats and had to be given a police escort when she attended the annual party conference.[117] Disgusted by the failure to act, a number of MPs (not only Jewish members) resigned from the party. During the subsequent General Election of December 2019, the identification of the Labour Party with anti-Semitism was raised as an issue. There is no knowing how much this influenced the outcome (in which Labour lost by a large margin) although it certainly reflected poorly on Corbyn's own character and performance as a leader.

In many ways, the response to Labour's recent bout of anti-Semitism demonstrates that the kind of treatment that has been evident since Corbyn took the reins is simply not acceptable in British society. Successive attempts by the Labour Party to clear its own name only worsened the situation. An internally commissioned, 850-page report was, effectively, ignored and it was left to an independent body to intervene. Thus, in May 2019, the UK's Equality and Human Rights Commission announced that it would be conducting its own wide-ranging investigation into whether Labour 'unlawfully discriminated against, harassed or victimised people because they are Jewish'.[118] The short answer is that this was exactly what they were doing. The wording in the report could not be plainer.[119] Labour had repeatedly broken the law and caused untold offence to Jews within the political party and more widely. From the evils of Zionism to the machinations of Jewish bankers, all of the old canards of anti-Semitism could be heard again. That was bad enough in itself, but what really cut to the chase was that the leadership of the party had done nothing to punish the offenders nor to prevent it continuing. Even, or especially, the previous leader, Jeremy Corbyn, was without remorse. When presented with the findings he could see no reason to apologize and the new leader of the party, Sir Keir Starmer, had no option but to suspend him from the party.

There is no doubt, if only to secure its own credibility, that there will be root and branch changes within the Labour Party to make sure that nothing of this sort can happen again. Although the whole business leaves a bitter taste, it also encourages a more optimistic response. In an article appropriately headed 'Anti-Semitism and the two sides of Britain' one observer reminds his readers that this is not Germany in the 1930s:

> *This is the country of the anti-Semitic writer GK Chesterton but also of the incomparably greater writer, the philosemitic George Eliot. It's the country of Jeremy Corbyn but also of Keir Starmer. And, here in Britain, as we have just found out once more, it is almost always the latter who wins out.*[120]

So, where does this recent episode leave my own relatives? They all came to England, mostly over the past two hundred years, in the hope of finding sanctuary. And, overall, the move to this country worked well. Given the history of how Jews were treated in the course of the diaspora, no-one could reasonably have expected that anti-Semitism would simply disappear. But, to date, when they have had to respond, right has been on their side. The evidence suggests that, if people stand up for themselves, an English sense of fairness will prevail. So long as there is free speech and a democratic government, there is a fair chance that decency and common sense will win the day. England has proved a good country to be our home, as the following words of a recent prime minister affirm:

> *I would be heartbroken if I ever thought that people in the Jewish community thought that Britain was no longer a safe place for them.*[121]

Chapter 9

Next Year in Jerusalem

Each year, the Passover service (the seder) ends with the head of the household intoning the solemn declaration, 'Next year in Jerusalem'. And all around the table, the gathering (usually a family but often with guests) repeats the pledge. Sometimes there are tears in the eyes of those who recall past suffering in the diaspora and allow themselves a glimpse of hope for their own generation. It is a poignant moment to end the service and one that is never forgotten.

Such is the shorthand version of what it means. It may have to be explained to young members of the family that this utterance predates, by nearly 2000 years, the formation in 1948 of the state of Israel. This is not a literal commitment to migrate. Instead, it is a thought embedded deep in the minds of every Jew who was forced, in that distant era, to leave their 'homeland' – a land that is symbolic as well as real but always represented by the ancient city of Jerusalem. That is where the long-awaited Messiah will come when the time is right; it is the place where the Temple, demolished by the Romans in the year 70, will be rebuilt; it is the allegorical city on a hill, a beacon of hope. Just in case there is any doubt about its importance, the words derived from the Pentateuch place Jerusalem in the centre of the universe:

> *The Land of Israel is the centre of the world: Jerusalem is the centre of the Land; the Holy Temple is the centre of Jerusalem; the Holy of Holies is the centre of the Holy Temple; the Holy Ark is the centre of the Holy of Holies and the Foundation Stone from which the world was established is before the Holy Ark.*[122]

Throughout the diaspora, the very thought of Jerusalem gave strength to the beleaguered Jews, as they journeyed from one country to another, in search of a place they could call home. Then, in the wake of horrendous suffering in the Second Word War, their call for salvation was answered, a new homeland was created. It drew to it the remnants of a once-large population from central and eastern Europe; it provided refuge for the many Jews in the Arab world, forced to flee from an unfriendly populace opposed to the new nation; and it later offered an escape route for Jews still living in Russia, who feared that they might once again be subject to a new wave of persecution. But for most Jews it failed to be the answer. In spite of annually repeating the mantra, 'Next year in Jerusalem', the record shows that very few left their homes in the West, my own family included. Why, when the prize was presented on a golden plate, was the offer not accepted? Why was Israel seen as the panacea for some but not others? Why did my own family turn its back on the opportunity to 'return' to the Promised Land, *Eretz Israel*? Could it be that the 'homeland' was no longer seen as home?

Eretz Israel

A fairer paradise is founded now
For Adam and his chosen sons, whom thou
A savior art come down to reinstall,
Where they shall dwell secure.[123]

The idea that Israel is the Promised Land and Jews the chosen people is a battleground of ideas. For some, the idea of exclusivity is to be found in the Torah, a literal prescription for the Jewish people; for others, it was less a question of religious dogma and more one of pragmatism, a means of survival; and, as an offshoot of the last of these, it was the emotion engendered by the Holocaust which added strength to the idea. Nor is that all, as, to add to the mix, the indigenous Palestinian population saw the Jewish claim as no more than a land grab by another name. Under the banner of Zion, the battle still rages; some Jews believe unequivocally that Israel is where the future lies; others have doubts. Jews who presently live outside the homeland are as numerous as those within. Each side invokes right in its armoury and, with none relenting, the issue remains unresolved, a perennial source of debate and dispute.

It all started a long time ago – in a region where boundaries were indeterminate, where any semblance of ethnic coherence was confounded by the existence of twelve nomadic tribes, and where stronger neighbours undermined attempts to bring stability. It was a troubled region then, as it is now. Broadly, the twelve Jewish tribes – united, if at all, by the pronouncements of Moses and the moral code of the Ten Commandments – settled across a wide area, known as the Land of Canaan, within which were the two provinces of Judaea and Israel. That the people were known as the Children of Israel defined them to the present day.

Religious Ordinance

To look first at the Torah, the earliest rabbis wrestled with interpretations of the word of God, brought to the people through the personage of Moses. Are these scholarly outcomes what God really intended? Certainly, if one is to read the opening lines of the Book of Joshua, in the Hebrew bible, that is what it seems:

> *... now therefore arise, go over this Jordan, thou, and all this people, unto the land which I do give to them, even to the children of Israel. Every place that the sole of your foot shall tread upon, that have I given unto you, as I said unto Moses. From the wilderness and this Lebanon even unto the great river, the river Euphrates, all the land of the Hittites, and unto the great sea toward the going down of the sun, shall be your coast.* [124]

But even in this categorical instruction, geography is not what it seems. To extend the territory to the banks of the Euphrates takes one well beyond what is later thought of as the Promised Land. The River Jordan offers a more limited but also (based on earlier patterns of settlement) a more realistic boundary to mark the area inhabited by the ancient Jews, yet even this is still disputed.

Clearly, in this interpretation (no matter the precise boundaries) the Jews were favoured by God. Even more so were the various allusions to the 'chosen people'. Was this God's reward for their early commitment to monotheism, putting their undying trust and love in just one deity?

> *For you are a people holy to the Lord your God; the Lord your God has chosen you to be a people for his own possession, out of all the peoples that are on the face of the earth... You shall be blessed above all peoples.* [125]

There can be little doubt that to be marked out as special, and with the prospect of returning one day to the land they were forced to leave, will have sustained the Jews on their seemingly endless travels during the diaspora. They would have received little enough encouragement or love from the host nations where they settled, in most cases temporarily; to know that at least they were privileged by God might have given them heart when it seemed that all else had failed. But there was also a price to pay. To be held up as the recipients of God's preferential treatment was hardly going to endear them to all those other races and religions that were not so favoured. Jews have been consistently disliked and harassed, not least of all because they assume this sense of superiority.

For believers in the literal word of the Hebrew bible, the related ideas of the 'chosen people' and the 'Promised Land' are unquestionable. But *why* should those of a less orthodox bent adopt this view? For the critical mind (and that includes not simply outsiders who reject the idea of Israel, but also sceptics within the faith) the bible is self-justifying. To coin a modern catch-phrase, 'they would say that, wouldn't they'. The very idea can provoke as much as it resolves; there is surely too much doubt in the argument to prove the case. As a result, other views prevail.

A Way to Survive

In spite of God's promise for the future, two thousand years is a long time to endure repeated persecution in one form or another. It seemed not to matter whether Jews assimilated in the country where they settled, following the customs of the host society, the outcome was always the same: they were regarded as aliens and simply not wanted as neighbours and compatriots.

So what was the answer? Religious belief had always offered a sense of hope, a constant in a sea of change. Even, too, a sense of identity; but, so experience showed, nothing more. It was time to look for a different solution, one that would enable the race to survive. Being a cuckoo in the nest had not worked. Was the way forward, instead, to build one's own nest? The answer came in the form of Zionism.

Instead of focusing only on religion, the Zionists switched attention to the idea of a Jewish nation state. The movement gathered pace towards the end of the nineteenth century, with the main branch finally abandoning the idea that national identity and security could be achieved within the diaspora. A country within a country was not enough. Instead, there must be separation from other nations and (finding common ground with the religious lobby) a new state should be formed where it had all started, in the old land of Palestine. Zion was one of the two hills in Jerusalem, but it came to mean Jerusalem the city, Jerusalem the Promised Land. The choice of place was symbolic but clear; that was where the new nation would be based.

Towards the end of the nineteenth century, under the leadership of luminaries like Theodor Herzl and, later, Chaim Weizmann, the new movement gathered pace. Networks were established and Zionists built a convincing case amongst politicians and international diplomats. It was not surprising that the initial impetus for the movement came from Russia and eastern Europe, where Jews were suffering most at the time, but gradually the axis shifted towards the west. With the demise of the Ottoman Empire, the First World War was pivotal in changing the balance of power in the region where Palestine was located. Britain assumed a mandate to govern the contentious territory and, therefore, became the lynch pin in any future negotiations. While it worked in favour of the Zionist cause to be rid of Ottoman opposition, it was not to help that Britain courted support from the Arabs during the war itself. There was even talk (encouraged by the legendary T.E. Lawrence) of creating a pan-Arab nation to extend over much of the Middle East. For the Zionists, the rise of Arab nationalism was the last thing that was wanted at that crucial stage. In fact, Britain was not averse to backing two horses to win the same race and, even before the war ended, the then Foreign Secretary announced what is eponymously known as the Balfour Declaration. The negotiations behind the scenes were complex and intense but the resultant message was plain for all to read:

> *His Majesty's government view with favour the establishment in Palestine of a national home for the Jewish people.*[126]

The Jews celebrated; the Arabs declared it would never happen. Britain had lit the blue touch paper and there was no turning back. Yet a Jewish state was by no means, at that point, a done deal. Much was still to happen before it was. While the politicians argued, practical steps were taken; pioneer settlers bought land from Arab owners and set about taming the arid countryside. So long as numbers were relatively small, tensions were kept within bounds. But as numbers increased, the Zionist plans posed a growing threat to the Arabs. The case for a separate state was strong in itself but, without the understanding if not also the support of the non-

Jewish population in Palestine, it would only store up problems for the future. At this formative stage, more needed to be done in an attempt to bring all parties on side, no matter how difficult that would be.

Emotional Groundswell

It is likely that the case for a Jewish nation state would have been argued, backwards and forwards, for years to come. Intrepid pioneers would have continued to buy land, legitimately, from non-Jewish owners, but always the eventual outcome would be in doubt. For every argument put forward by the Zionists, the Arabs would argue to the contrary. In the voting chambers of international bodies this would almost certainly yield a stalemate. If America voted in favour, its rivals would vote against; if Britain invoked the spirit of Balfour, they would be reminded of the part of the declaration which guaranteed the interests of Palestine's indigenous population. And so it would have gone on.

But, in the event, something happened which triggered a momentous change. Hitler, in his demented desire to rid the world of all Jews, inadvertently secured their survival. Not all of them, not by a long way, with nearly six million systematically murdered in the concentration camps in the Second World War. Of those who entered the camps there were few survivors, but when the world finally confronted what had happened, the sight of emaciated bodies and uncomprehending eyes would touch even the most resistant souls. This was no time for age-old chants of anti-Semitism. For a short while at least, intellectual and political opposition fell into the background and unadulterated emotion came to the fore. It is not often that empathy wins the day in the calculating environment of the geopolitical arena, but this was one of the rare moments when it did.

Understandably, the Zionists thought their time had finally come. They lobbied fiercely for international support and, anticipating that Britain, still trying to please all parties, would not be a reliable ally, they correctly switched their prime allegiance to the United States. In terms of having the power to bring in other nations too, that was a good move and America remained a strong friend in the years to come. When, in November 1947, it came to the vote in the recently-formed United Nations, 33 voted in favour of the new state of Israel, 13 against and 10 abstained. Amongst the abstaining nations was Britain, hoist by its own petard of trying to favour equally both Jews and Arabs. Britain lost its mandate in the process and its reputation was further damaged by its actions in turning back boatloads of desperate Jewish immigrants, fleeing from a devastated continent. The nation paid dearly for its duplicitous attempt to please both sides. All of the other western nations, and America's worldwide allies, voted in favour, as did the USSR.

Inheriting what by then seemed the impossible task of making it all work, the UN called for a partition plan, with the coveted prize of Jerusalem put under an international trusteeship. The boundaries, designed to separate the two new nations, were Byzantine – zig-zagging their way around existing pockets of settlement and never likely to be upheld. Sure enough, the Arab lobby bitterly opposed the arrangement and, as soon as independence was declared, their armies sought to drive the newcomers into the sea. In the face of fierce resistance by the Israelis, they failed to do so. But the tone was set for the subsequent history of the region, one of repeated wars and terrorist acts. Attempts to find a lasting solution have evaded successive world leaders. It had been the constant hope of Jews that the establishment of their own state would release them from the insecurity they had known throughout the diaspora. But, as the record shows, that was not to be. The Zionist case was strong, helped by a groundswell of emotion. But the Arab case was also strong and there has since been a failure to bridge the gulf between the two sides. Subsequent wars have failed to resolve the problem and repeated diplomatic initiatives have been equally unsuccessful.

Local Objections

The underlying problem was that the land that the Jews long ago felt compelled to leave, and which they vowed to return to, was also the home of Arab tribes who had been there at the time of the original settlement. But when the Jews left the Arabs stayed, continuing the way of life they had always known. It was a largely pastoral existence, mixed with small-scale farming, although there was also fishing and sea-borne trade along the eastern Mediterranean coastline. Most of the indigenous population would have known little about the fate of the departed Jews until towards the end of the nineteenth century, when a small number returned to what they regarded as their lost homeland. Arab landowners were at first mystified when the incomers offered them a fair price for their meagre holdings, but they accepted willingly. Only gradually, as numbers increased, was there growing anxiety, based on a fear that the dispossessed Arabs might one day become a minority.

By 1925 the number of new settlers was 108,000, rising to 235,000 in 1933, the year that Hitler came to power; in the following years the rate of increase accelerated, to a point where the British introduced restrictions to appease the Arabs who feared being overwhelmed. Yet, even amidst growing concerns amongst both parties contesting the land – marked by a series of riots and general unrest – the sale of holdings continued. It was a legitimate process and was later to undermine the argument of the Arabs that the Jews had wrongly appropriated their land for their own nationalistic purpose. On the eve of the creation of the new state, Jewish immigrants comprised 30% of the total population.

When the United Nations met in New York in 1947 to mediate a resolution, it had before it what was to prove one of its most formidable challenges. On the one side, the Zionists had the wind in their sails and were determined not to give way when their destination was in sight; while the Arabs, in turn, were bitterly opposed to the proposed partition of what they saw as their own land and the resultant creation of a Jewish state in their midst. They did their best in the international forum to decouple the emotional argument about displaced and damaged Jews in Europe:

> *The question of Palestine is altogether independent and separate from the question of persecuted persons of Europe. The Arabs of Palestine are not responsible in any way for the persecution of the Jews in Europe. That persecution is condemned by the whole civilized world, and the Arabs are among those who sympathize with the persecuted Jews. However, the solution of that problem cannot be said to be a responsibility of Palestine, which is a tiny country and which has taken enough of those refugees and other people since 1920 … Any delegation which wishes to express its sympathy has more room in its country than has Palestine, and has better means of taking in these refugees and helping them.*[127]

Nor were the Palestinian Arabs alone in their bitter opposition, with their neighbours viewing with growing alarm the advent of a new nation with the potential to grow well beyond its initial size, becoming no less than 'a bridgehead against the Arab world'.[128]

Little wonder, shortly before it came to the vote, the UN could report that 'the atmosphere in Palestine today is one of profound tension'.[129] Given the intensity of feeling, a democratic vote in a distant part of the world was hardly going to change that. Arab intentions were barely below the surface and, sure enough, on the very day following the announcement of the independent state of Israel, the neighbouring nations of Egypt, Jordan, Iraq, Syria and Lebanon united with the Palestinians to turn back the clock. After fierce fighting and the loss of many lives, the various attacks were repelled and Israel lived to see another day. For the Arabs, though, there was the added pain of large numbers fleeing their homes to live in refugee camps across the various borders. It was a costly battle and certainly not the last of these regional wars, requiring Israel to be permanently well-armed and always on its guard. Any hopes that a return to the homeland would end the uncertainties of the diaspora were immediately dispelled and, in more than seven decades since its inception, the situation has not improved. Israel remains day-by-day on war alert, by now with the threatening presence of Iran amongst its foremost enemies.

Aliyah and Allah

This land is your land, and this land is my land…
This land was made for you and me.[130]

Sadly, the charm and simplicity of Woody Guthrie's lyric failed to carry as far as the eastern Mediterranean. If it were not for the intransigence of politicians and a general unwillingness amongst all parties to adapt to the new situation, the idea of 'your land' and 'my land' might just have worked. Instead, the very thought of sharing in this vexed region seems beyond comprehension to those who live there, and each side justifies its position with an immutable sense of righteousness. But why?

Judaism and Islam are different religions, but not so far apart that they have been unable to live together in the past. Many Jews thrived under Ottoman rule, steering a manageable line between what was permissible and what was not. There was room for both sides to prosper. Just as they did at the time of the Moors in Spain, until the Catholics regained control and the large population of Jews was expelled from the whole of the Iberian Peninsula. Culturally, too, Arabs and Jews have much in common. They both hold the family unit in high regard, their language has the same Semitic roots, and even their diets, in what they both regard as their homeland, are remarkably similar. And yet the two peoples are constantly divided, starkly illustrated now by a colossal wall, snaking its way along the length of the country. For the Israelis (who built it), the structure is seen as a security fence, while for the Arabs it is regarded as an apartheid barrier. In their contrasting ways, both are right, just as those who portray the wall as evidence of a seemingly irreconcilable divide between the two sides are right too. This is not what was anticipated when Jews dreamed of one day 'coming home'.

Aliyah is a keyword in the lexicon of Zionism, referring to the age-old wish to return to the land of Israel. Throughout the long history of the diaspora it remained in the forefront of prayers and discussion, sometimes expressed as 'the act of going up' to encompass the idea of Jerusalem as a higher place. Had the state of Israel been established towards the end of the nineteenth century – when the Zionist movement was still taking shape – it is likely that the number of immigrants would have been many times more than was later the case. Instead, with Israel not yet an option, most of those who left Europe went to North America. Just as was the case for the smaller number who settled in England, within a generation or two these places became home. After what was often a difficult start, they were getting good jobs, buying houses and, not least of all, living without the daily fear of persecution. Why would they then wish to leave all that behind in order to start afresh in a hostile environment, a country which, on its first day of nationhood, was attacked from all sides by enemies vowing to end the dream? That seemed too much like the world from which they had so recently escaped.

On setting out to write this book, I knew that one of the questions to be answered was why, in spite of a genuine sense of support for Israel, not a single one of my close relatives went to settle there. But if the question was posed in a different way, the answer soon became apparent. The real issue was not to ask why our families did not fulfil the dream of *Aliyah*, but, on the contrary, why would they? Surely after centuries of searching, the fact is that they had at last found what they were looking for. Every Friday evening – in a New York apartment or a London suburb – families would gather to light candles, say prayers and share a traditional dinner. The children would tell of what they had done at school in the week and talk about their friends. On the sabbath they could walk in peace to their chosen synagogue, without fear of abuse or attack. Attending bar mitzvahs and weddings, as well as celebrating the main religious festivals together, was an important part of their social calendar. They lived close to others in their community, but not exclusively so. They were also part of a wider society. For north Londoners, going to watch Spurs or Arsenal on a

Sunday afternoon added to their sense of belonging. There was something missing, of course, the spiritual sense of belonging that would have come with migrating to the Promised Land, fulfilling the promise of earlier generations. But, on balance, it seemed like a reasonable compromise.

This kind of decision to stay where they were, made by a multitude of individuals across the world, is reflected in the demographics of contemporary Jewry. It is estimated that there are currently close to 15 million Jews in total. This compares with 16.6 million, the highest recorded number in their history, on the eve of the Second World War. With the decimation of so many during the war itself, the total fell to little more than 11 million by 1945, 650,000 of whom had already settled in what was still the mandated territory of Palestine. In spite of the difficulties confronting the new state of Israel, the population of Jews in the country increased, year on year. It now totals close to 7 million (45% of the world total), most of whom were born there. The United States comes next, with 5.7 million, together with sizeable minorities in France, Canada, the UK, Argentina, Russia, Germany and Australia.[131] Although, in this context, the diaspora is by no means consigned to history, it no longer has the negative connotations that marked it for two millennia.

From the time of its inception, the doors of Israel have been open to anyone who can show that they are Jewish. A law to that effect was passed in 1950, the Law of Return. Israel offered salvation to emigrés from Europe at the end of the war, and from Russia and Ukraine when they were permitted to leave in large numbers in the 1990s. Many Jews came, too, from North Africa and from Arab nations in the Middle East, as well as Orthodox communities from around the world, convinced that it was the right thing to do. But, still, more Jews have chosen to live in countries other than the Promised Land. Nor could they be easily persuaded to do otherwise. They are no longer compelled to disperse but this is what many have chosen to do; the modern diaspora has become a product of free will.

Partly to give doubters a taste of what they were missing, and to encourage more of the Jewish diaspora to make Israel their home, a novel scheme was adopted to enable young people to spend a few months working on a kibbutz. The scheme is well known and over the years has attracted large numbers of volunteers to the country's pioneer settlements, including two of my own family (then of student age), my daughter Gemma and elder son Rowan.

Hardy

Dawn on the West Bank

Gemma Hardy recalls:
I worked in Kibbutz Gilgal, on the West Bank about 15 minutes' drive from Jerusalem. It was a small kibbutz. One of its attractions for volunteers was that it didn't have a factory. Instead, jobs included working in the kitchen/dining room (this seemed to be mostly for the really long-term volunteers and was considered quite a privilege); in the vineyards (where one day we had to be on our best behaviour when buyers from Marks & Spencer visited); on the date plantation (great fun going up in cherry pickers to pick dates and climbing precariously amongst the waving palms, plus eating some of the delicious, sweet fruit warmed by the sun); in the mango plantation (where we had to wear long sleeves, trousers and rubber gloves to protect our skin from the potent juice that squirted out when we picked the mangoes and caused painful rashes); or the turkey sheds that absolutely stank. We would sometimes listen to an old transistor radio in the vineyards where we could pick up the World Service. We heard old radio plays that may have been recorded decades ago, with actors speaking in clipped BBC accents to remind us of home.

We got up at 5am and would climb sleepily into the tractor trailer to be driven into the fields by Doron, the very overweight and surly boss of the volunteers. We couldn't wait until breakfast at 9am, when we would fill up with carrots, cucumbers, eggs, yoghurt and jam – often all in the same bowl! When breakfast was over, those on dining-room duties would clean up, loading the industrial dishwashers and hosing down the floors with a strong-smelling detergent that looked like bright pink bubble gum. We all had our own laundry number and had to write in large letters with a permanent marker in every one of our clothes. I once handwashed some red trousers and left them to dry, draped over an enormous cactus, in the scorching sun. The strength of the sun bleached one side pink and the cactus left a series of small holes in them. I could only ever wear them to work in the fields afterwards.

For entertainment, we had a wonderful outdoor swimming pool, Friday-night discos in the bomb shelter, or the very occasional trip into Jerusalem where we would treat ourselves to fantastic falafel. Most of the Israelis on the kibbutz kept a polite distance, probably because it wasn't worth investing time in people who stayed for such a short time. My experience of the kibbutz was one of hard work, and I came home feeling fit and strong. I made some good friends – two of whom I'm still in touch with – and thoroughly enjoyed my time there.

Gemma is one of many who enjoyed the experience but was not persuaded to stay. Her own Promised Land lay elsewhere. The fact is that for those who saw the scheme as an opportunity to find out more about Israel, the kibbutz was no longer typical of the rest of the nation. In the pioneering days (even before the establishment of Israel) a kibbutz spoke eloquently of building – and defending – the Promised Land together.

Driven by strong socialist principles, the collective reigned over the individual; property was shared, as were goals. The kibbutz was a means to an end. Yet, ironically, the more it succeeded in providing one of the essential building blocks of the new state, the less it became relevant. After a hesitant start, Israel looked for its main support to the United States and the West rather than what might have seemed the more ideologically aligned socialism of the Soviet bloc. And the more the country veered towards a mixed economy with a welfare state, the more the kibbutz became an anachronism.

Historically, though, it remains one of the most important experiments in communal living, and probably also one of the best documented.[132] And for volunteers it still offered a unique insight into the life of the nation, bringing home both the biblical connections that survived in local place names, and the immediacy of Middle East politics.

Hardy

River of Life

Rowan Hardy writes:
I volunteered to work in Kibbutz Gesher, just south of the Sea of Galilee. The farmland ran down to the River Jordan, which flowed beyond the minefield and razor wire of the border fence between Israel and its neighbour with the same name as the river. I was very fortunate to work in the irrigation team, which maintained an ingenious system of pipes and sprinklers, giving life to fields of corn, avocado and herbs like oregano and basil. Thanks to the plentiful water from the river, crops grew well in the difficult conditions.

We started early to avoid the burning heat of the day. It was still dark as we drove down into the fields in trucks and tractors, loaded with huge tanks of cool water to keep us refreshed. As we started work, the sun rose over the Jordanian mountains behind us. From our lush fields, dripping with water, sometimes I would hear a local goatherd across the border calling to his flock, and I would even catch the pungent scent of his goats in the morning air.

As the heat of the morning built up, we would soak each other with the hoses and sprinklers and drink litres of cool water. Driving the tractors was fun and we soon picked up the skills from long-time volunteers and our Israeli hosts. One of the old tractors had a crackling radio and on some mornings we would tune into the BBC World Service as we worked: home seemed very far away.

We returned to the kibbutz for a huge breakfast of fresh fruits, vegetables and cheese, before completing our work by lunchtime. The afternoons were spent resting and swimming in the beautiful pool. Sometimes, when the day became cooler, we would cycle up to the Sea of Galilee, enjoying a welcome Maccabee beer in Big Ben's bar.

Conclusion

The Past is a Foreign Country

The geographer, David Lowenthal, wrote a seminal book on our understanding of the past and the modern obsession with heritage.[133] He takes as his title the words of the English novelist, L.P. Hartley, 'The past is a foreign country', who in his own writing adds the rest of the sentence: 'they do things differently there'.[134]

L.P Hartley was absolutely right, and in the the context of this 'family history' these are wise words that I have tried constantly to bear in mind. What was done in the past cannot easily be compared with the present. The actions of my ancestors can best be understood in the context that prevailed at the time. Glib comparisons between past and present are to be avoided. But we can at least describe what we discover.

We know, for instance, that Nathan Nathan and Joseph Moses were both convicted of crimes that led to their separate transportations from the East End of London to the new colony of Australia. We know that the hardships endured became opportunities to turn around their lives. And we know that they were both, by any standards, remarkably successful in creating timely businesses that thrived in the emergent colonies. Their stories are rightly prominent on the preceding pages and deserve to be told and retold as models of resilience and human endeavour.

Nor is it only a story of business success, as it was rooted, no less, in the total commitment of their families. Their many children, as well as brothers and sisters, followed in their footsteps and changed their own lives too, not to mention helping to build Jewish communities on the far side of the world. In any age, their various stories would challenge credulity, bordering, in what they did, on fiction rather than real life.

This line of the Moss family was exceptional, but there are other strands of family history which have also claimed attention. It was a brave decision, for instance, of Jacob Elia Abdela to leave the shores of the Ionian Sea to start a new life for him and his young family in the alien surroundings of Manchester. His children all fared well and, as we have seen, one of his sons, Isaac, was to gain a deserved reputation as a builder of boats. In turn, Isaac's own son, Fred, later made a name for himself in the world of catering.

Then there were the various women who refused to accept that their religion (and, indeed, social norms at the time) had assigned them to a secondary role. When our ancestors sat apart from the men in the synagogue, who knows what they were thinking? What impelled Rosetta Nathan, for example, to combine life as a homemaker with the strength to support her husband's business in a faraway land? And, to bring it up to date, what led Lesley Abdela away from the world of business, in which the men in her family had excelled for several generations, and to carve a career for herself in championing women's rights? Women have shown enormous strength, not only in high-profile roles like the above but also in holding their families together during the long days of the diaspora.

This short conclusion is not the place to repeat the many stories that have already been told. But it is a reminder of the debt that is owed by present generations to the pioneers of the past. Their lives were not easy and, in looking back, we have indeed ventured into a foreign country. But not everything was so different. Many of the values we can see there are recognizable and perhaps, too, a source of inspiration for the present, if not the future. It is tempting to think in these terms and to look ahead with hope that one day there will be more of the same to report. Yet the reality is that the future is surely even more foreign than the past.

In spite of numerous think-tanks and predictive models, we simply have no idea of what lies ahead. The experience of living through a largely-unexpected global pandemic that burst upon the scene in 2020 is proof enough of that. As a result, this journey into the past ends on what some will see as a discordant note. One thing that for so long bound all Jews together, during the whole of the diaspora, was an undying belief in their shared identity. It is beyond question that their religion and race made all of our ancestors what they were, whatever the cost in terms of their livelihoods and the vulnerabilities they endured as a result. And in the collective mind was always the ethereal image of Jerusalem, the city on a hill that symbolized what they had left and to which one day they would return. 'Next year in Jerusalem' helped every Jew to keep going in the face of adversity.

But all of that is no more. From around the middle of the past century, the world has experienced far-reaching change. The state of Israel was formed in 1948, but this in itself was not the decisive factor in Jewish life. During this modern period, a mere seventy years or so, the map of family life has been redrawn, as has our attachment to national identity and, not least of all, the importance of religious worship. Jews are still fiercely loyal to who they are, never more so than in the face of anti-Semitism. That is as it has always been. And yet now there are vast differences too. Whereas once the very idea of 'marrying out' was alien to core beliefs, this practice is now commonplace; whereas previously the various host countries, where Jews lived, restricted what they could do, now (at least beyond the Arab world) there are no limits to assimilation; and whereas for millennia the dream of 'returning' to the homeland was beyond contention, most of the Jewish population in the world have made the choice to live in countries other than Israel.

So what does all this mean for modern Judaism? It means that many, perhaps most, Jews are no longer driven by the knowledge of who they are and commitment to a common cause. They are English as well as Jewish; their home is in Buenos Aires as well as Tel Aviv; some are critics of the state of Israel, while others remain ardent Zionists. There is no unanimity, as there was more likely to have been in the past, and my own family reflects something of this extraordinary mix that has taken its place. This is neither a cause for disappointment nor celebration, merely an observation on how things have changed.

We can look back with pride at how our ancestors coped with difficult situations, but our own lives are in the here and now. If this family history reveals anything it is that Jews have shown themselves to be remarkably adaptable. They have evolved in order to survive. And, no doubt, in different ways again, something of this constant process of evolution will continue. The form this will take now is very largely out of the hands of the older generations; we might, at most, share our thoughts and understanding of the past. We would be exceeding our brief, however, to administer instruction. It will be in the hands of the younger family members to make decisions that will take them into what is still uncharted territory. The past is ours, the future is theirs.

This book has offered no more than a glimpse of what it is like to be Jewish in England. It would take a brave soul, or a foolish one, to say what it will be like tomorrow.

Afterword

At the risk of resembling a hefty government report, which ends with the words 'more research needs to be done', this is exactly how I intend to conclude this book. No-one can be more aware than I am that there are gaps to be filled, more lines of enquiry to be followed. But in the course of research and writing for this particular volume, an enormous amount of work has been done and a forest of family trees has been planted. For those who would like to pursue this, all of our findings have been placed on the invaluable website and search engine *ancestry.com*. This is a subscription-based website; however, if you are not a member, access can be provided temporarily by invitation. Please contact the author via *bluegeckobooks@ymail.com* for further information.

As I have previously explained, this book has not been intended as a conventional family history and there is a reason why it has been done in this way. But it is not to say that unacknowledged details of past and current generations of the many different families involved are unimportant, nor is it to suggest that they are without general interest. Some families get little more than a mention, but each lineage has a new and fascinating story to tell, subject matter for a wealth of other books! If family members choose to complete the task, I hope the generalized narrative in this book will help to provide a context.

Compass Points

In the main text I have tried to keep personal family history at bay. Reference is made to various ancestors but only for what they can tell us about general trends and particular events. Only now am I making an exception, by bringing together some of the details of my four grandparents; many of these details are already dotted around in the text but it might be useful, now, to collate them in this way.

I knew that if I started with my grandparents, I would be able to make connections with everyone else referred to later. In the complex web of an extended family, grandparents provide essential departure points. These, for me, are the four points of the compass, giving direction to the various journeys into the past.

The reader can be reminded that my paternal grandfather was Simon (known as Sam) Hardy (originally Hardy Simon) and that he married Julia Goodman; while my maternal grandmother was Sophia (known as Birdie) Moss, married to Isaac Abdela. The four given names combined to produce two continuing family trees: the Hardys and the Abdelas. An unusual twist is that a brother of one of these two families (Harry Hardy) married a sister from the other (Violet Abdela), and *vice versa* (Fred Abdela married Etta Hardy).

For added interest, the threads which bind them together draw on both the Sephardi and Ashkenazi traditions of Jewish culture, not to mention the lesser-known Romaniotes who claim a direct lineage with the original homeland of Jews in the eastern Mediterranean.

Hardy/Goodman

When Sam married Julia...

Hardy Simon was his full name but he was usually known as Sam. Like many Jews in England in the interwar period, he wanted something that sounded less Jewish and, at some point after 1929, he changed his original name from Hardy Simon to Simon Hardy. Families from central and eastern Europe who were only too aware of the realities of persecution were not prepared to take unnecessary risks in their new country of adoption. In both world wars there was, too, strong anti-German sentiment in Britain, so a name change would help to remove any confusion about loyalties.

Sam was born in Hanover (in what was then Prussia) in 1881, to Max and Ida Simon (née Hoffmann). His father owned a pianoforte factory but, while Sam's was still a boy, the family decided to close shop and move to England, settling at various addresses in north-west London. For a short period they moved out of the metropolis, across the Lee Valley, to take up residence in the rural setting of Theydon Bois in Essex. But country life was obviously not to their liking and they soon returned to the suburbs.

The original move from Germany to England seems to have taken place when he was quite young; one of his sisters was born in this country when Sam was only eight. There were five children in the family – three sons and two daughters. The youngest of the family, Bernhard, would later leave England to make a career for himself in the emergent film industry in Hollywood. He was known there as Jeffrey Bernerd, one of a pioneering generation of film-makers.

At the age of twelve, when the family home was in Brondesbury, Sam attended the nearby St Augustine's School. It seems that his father had returned to his former trade as a pianoforte manufacturer and that Sam joined him. At the age of thirty, Sam was listed as the manager of a 'pianoforte and upholstery factory' in London's Holloway Road. There are few traces of his later career, although there are references to the film industry (a film company in Isleworth is mentioned in the records), and also a note that at one stage he was a bookie. On his death certificate his occupation is listed as 'Laboratory Attendant (retired)', and this may well have been in a film laboratory.

In 1905, with the prospect of a steady job working for his father, Sam married Julia Goodman. She was then only 19.

Her father, Joseph, came from Austria and her mother, Sarah Abrahams, from a family that had emigrated to England from Holland. While still a young girl, Julia and her parents moved away from the crowded inner-city community where she had been born; first to Hackney and then to Brondesbury. This kind of move proved to be a well-trodden path for many of the immigrant Jews, who settled first in the East End before finding their way to one of London's developing suburbs (usually to the north and east of the capital).

There is no evidence of how Sam and Julia met, but around that time they were living in the same part of London. Sam might simply have set eyes on her in passing or, perhaps, they both attended the same social or religious event. Either way, marriage was not long delayed and by 1911 the records show that they were already the parents of four daughters – Henrietta, Josephine, Ida and Trixie – with their only son, Harry, born later in that same year. When two of the sisters married in 1931, they were using the surname of Hardy. Trixie was not married until 1942 but, for one reason or another, was still registered as Simon.

Like so many others of that generation, however, they were denied the opportunity to bring up their children in peace. Events on the Continent were soon to spiral out of control and in 1914 the first guns were fired to mark the start of the First World War. It is not clear whether Sam was called to service but the records show that a Private Hardy Simon enlisted with the locally-based Middlesex Regiment.

Sadly, Julia died in 1945 and we have little to record her life. I have only a vague recollection of being taken to meet her when she was an invalid confined to bed. With the passing of Julia, Sam lived as a widower for a further 16 years. During that period, I recall that he came regularly to my parents' flat in Kilburn for the Friday evening shabat dinner.

My mother invariably fried fish for the occasion, which Sam ate with relish. He was a portly gentleman who liked his food and would be dressed on those evenings in a three-piece suit with a tightly-buttoned waistcoat. After dinner, he would take off his jacket and play cards with my father, before setting off to catch a bus to take him home to his flat in Tottenham Street, in central London. It was there that he died, at the age of 80, as a result of heart disease and diabetes.

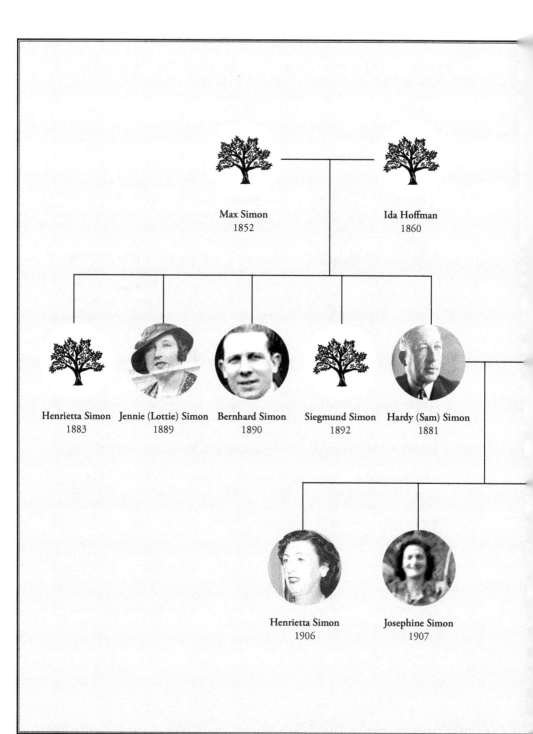

Max Simon
1852

Ida Hoffman
1860

Henrietta Simon
1883

Jennie (Lottie) Simon
1889

Bernhard Simon
1890

Siegmund Simon
1892

Hardy (Sam) Simon
1881

Henrietta Simon
1906

Josephine Simon
1907

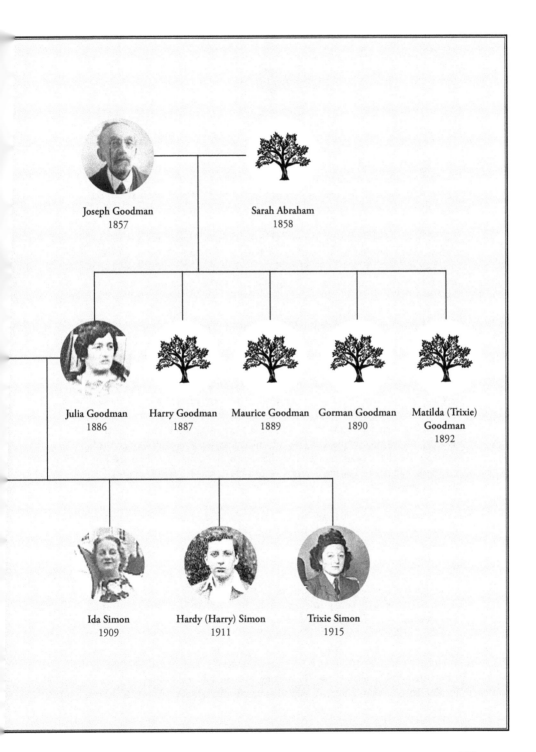

Joseph Goodman
1857

Sarah Abraham
1858

Julia Goodman
1886

Harry Goodman
1887

Maurice Goodman
1889

Gorman Goodman
1890

Matilda (Trixie)
Goodman
1892

Ida Simon
1909

Hardy (Harry) Simon
1911

Trixie Simon
1915

Abdela/Moss

...and Birdie Married Isaac

The other principal family – the Abdelas – is the result of another marriage between immigrants; this time with origins geographically far apart, with one set of relatives coming to England via Canada and the other from Corfu.

Sophia (known as 'Birdie') Moss was born in 1874 in Montreal, Canada. Her father, Joseph Edward Moss was himself born in the same Canadian city and her mother, Julia Rose Joseph, had migrated from Australia. Julia Rose was a daughter of Moses and Rosetta Joseph, who had earlier made their fortunes in New South Wales.

Against the flow of migration at the time, which was overwhelmingly from Europe to America, Birdie's family left Canada to set up a business in London. By then, their distant roots in the impoverished East End had been forgotten and they chose to live, instead, in a fashionable part of London. In 1881 her father was listed as an 'export merchant', living at 31 Westbourne Park with his wife and five children. The family was soon to move to a different address in west London, this time in Notting Hill. It must have been a substantial dwelling as, in addition to the seven members of the family, there was a governess, cook and housemaid. In 1901 they were still there, although by then Joseph was recorded as a retired shipping merchant. With the children that much older, the need for a resident governess had passed but there were now two parlour maids as well as the cook and housemaid.

Birdie's childhood sounds a happy one, living in the kind of middle-class, London home portrayed so well in J.M. Barrie's Peter Pan (though with no evidence in this case of a large dog to keep watch over the children). She was the oldest of five siblings, with three brothers, Melville, Clarence and Julian, and a sister, Rosalind.

Although Birdie was still living at home in 1901, just two years later she left to marry into a Sephardi family, originally from the Mediterranean island of Corfu. Her new husband, Isaac Abdela, had business interests centred in Manchester, and that is where they made their home.

Children soon arrived, although by the standards of the time just three would have been quite a small family. First came Miriam Julia (known as Iris), then Jacob Frederick (known as Fred) and Violet Esther Rosalind.

Birdie, Isaac and Julia

Their father, Isaac, was very active but his health always gave cause for concern. He was greatly overweight and it was not unknown for him to eat a large breakfast in bed, which included a more-than-generous portion of fried fish prepared by the cook. Birdie was by no means overweight but for much of her adult life she was treated for diabetes and this eventually led to her demise.

Young Fred was encouraged to go out and make his way in in the world, which he did very successfully. In contrast, Iris, the sister of Fred and Violet was denied a happy life. At the age of 20, she married Abraham Shashoua, nearly twice her age at the time. The Shashouas, originally from Baghdad, had established themselves in Manchester, specializing first in shipping cotton to the Middle East and also supplying antiquities from Mesopotamia to the British Museum. Sadness first struck the couple when Iris gave birth to a son, Jack, who was born with a congenital heart disease. Although he had a lovely nature, and unmet aspirations to be a great film producer, he was clearly disadvantaged. Tragically, Iris's husband was killed in a road accident in 1935 and a year later, at the age of 33, Iris took her own life. It was left to my mother and Birdie to make sure the bereft child (only ten years old at the time) was properly looked after. Much of my mother's early adulthood was spent in keeping watch over the health of her parents and caring for Jack.

Then, at the age of 56, Birdie's husband died. It was a premature death although Isaac had packed a lot into his relatively short life. He was an infant when he arrived in England in 1874 and grew up in a well-off family. But he had worked hard on his own account and became an accomplished engineer. He engaged in a number of activities before settling on shipbuilding, which is where he made his name, specializing in building river boats for export. At the peak of his activities, he employed as many as 700 workers.

After Isaac passed away, Birdie had no reason to remain in Manchester so returned to London with Violet, setting up home in Greencroft Gardens, between West Hampstead and Finchley Road. Like her previous homes, this was also a large house and her brother, Mellie (by then separated from his wife) and his son, Barry, lived there too, as did for a time her own son, Fred, with his new wife, Etta. There was another London move to come, this time along the Finchley Road to a flat in Morland Court, before moving with her daughter, Violet, to Brighton and then Hove. It was in the latter town that Birdie died, in 1945 at the age of 71.

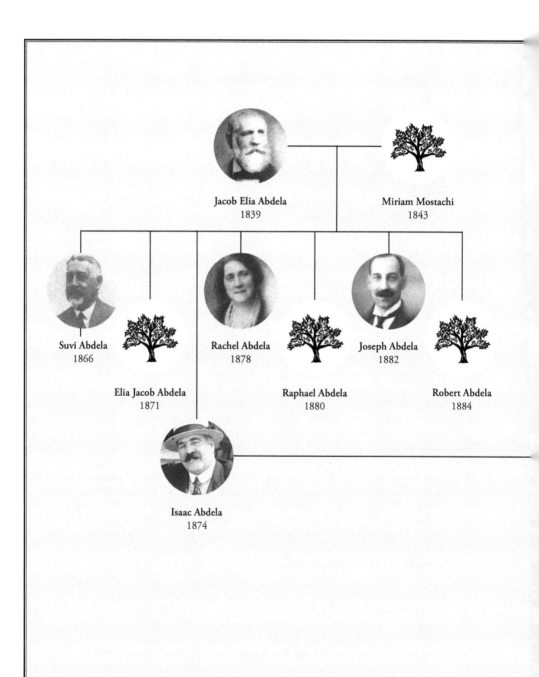

Jacob Elia Abdela
1839

Miriam Mostachi
1843

Suvi Abdela
1866

Rachel Abdela
1878

Joseph Abdela
1882

Elia Jacob Abdela
1871

Raphael Abdela
1880

Robert Abdela
1884

Isaac Abdela
1874

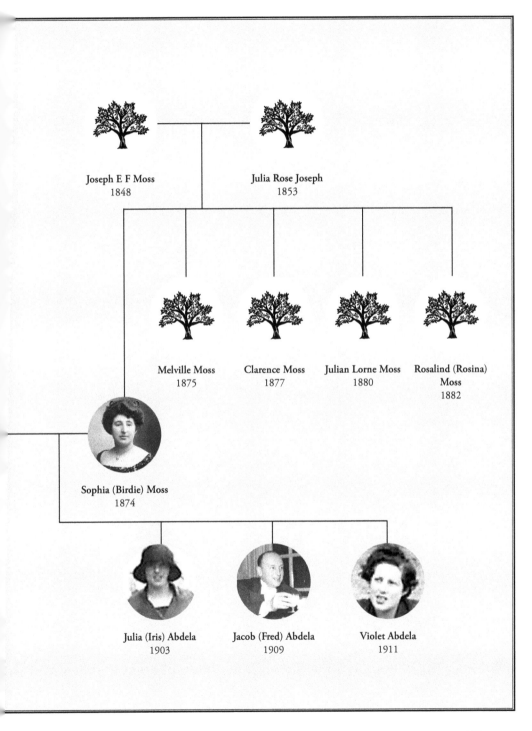

Joseph E F Moss
1848

Julia Rose Joseph
1853

Melville Moss
1875

Clarence Moss
1877

Julian Lorne Moss
1880

Rosalind (Rosina)
Moss
1882

Sophia (Birdie) Moss
1874

Julia (Iris) Abdela
1903

Jacob (Fred) Abdela
1909

Violet Abdela
1911

Notes and References

1   This chapter heading is, of course, a plundered version of *My Family and Other Animals*, a popular work by Gerald Durrell, the source of which I gratefully acknowledge.

2   *Jewish Encyclopaedia*, 1906. http://www.jewishencyclopedia.com articles/14773-wandering-jew

3   Pearl Buck, Peony, a novel published in 1948 that describes social barriers between the Chinese culture and that of the Kaifeng Jews.

4   Montefiore, S.S. (2011) *Jerusalem: The Biography*, London: Weidenfeld and Nicolson.

5   de Lange, N. (1984) *Atlas of the Jewish World*, Oxford: Phaidon Press.

6   Montefiore, *op.cit.*

7   de Lange, *op.cit.*

8   Genesis 17:8.

9   Johnson, P. (1987) *A History of the Jews*, New York: Harper & Row.

10 Benjamin of Tudela's diary was published as the *Book of Travels* and is noted in a short but interesting article, 'The Jews of Arta', by Constantinos A. Tsillyianni (trans. Marcia Ikonopoulos). https://616c76ef-bc6a-4949-877e-75b95e3c3fe0.filesusr.com ugd/0019a0_9bf175b4c0764dea87c2562e84c8a8eb.pdf

11 *Ibid.*

12 *The Jewish Chronicle*, 19 September 1902, cited in A.M. Langford, 'The steamboat builders of Brimscombe (Part 2)', Gloucestershire Society of Industrial Archaeology, 1988, pp.3-20.

13 Collins, L. (2006) *The Sephardim of Manchester: Pedigrees and Pioneers*, Manchester: Shaare Hayim. Her book is a model of meticulous scholarship, without which any history of the Jews in England would be much the poorer.

14 'Greece's last Romaniote's Jews remember a catastrophe', *Haaretz*, 4 April 2014. https://www.haaretz.com/jewish/greeces-last-romaniote-jews-1.5243995

15 de Lange, *op.cit.*

16 Dirk Hoerder, 'The Traffic of Emigration via Bremen/Bremerhaven: Merchants' interests, protective legislation, and migrants' experiences', *Journal of American Ethnic History*, Vol. 13, No. 1, Fall, 1993, pp.68-101.

17 Explanation in *Encyclopaedia Britannica*.

18 It was not just a question of lending money but also charging interest on the loans, known as the practice of usury and denied at the time to Christians.

19 Abrahams, B.L. (1895) *The Expulsion of the Jews from England in 1290*, Blackwell: Oxford. The essay first appeared in 1894 in the Jewish Quarterly Review.

20 Johnson, *op.cit.*

21 Zangwill, I. (1892) *Children of the Ghetto: A study of a peculiar people*, Jewish Publication Society of America.

22 Fishman, W.J. (1979) *The Streets of East London*, Duckworth: London.

23 Gathered from various sources: see, for instance, Rosemary O'Day, 'From diaspora to Whitechapel'. http://fathom.lse.ac.uk Features/122537/

24 Bermant, C. (1975) *Point of Arrival: A study of London's East End*, London: Eyre Methuen.

25 Well into the 1950s, one could still come across small shops with barrels of pickled cucumber and some with the ubiquitous herring, beloved of all who lived within reach of the Baltic.

26 Booth, C. (1889 and 1891) *Life and Labour of the People in London*, Vol.1, and *Labour and Life of the People in London*, Vol.2, London.

27 Zangwill, *op.cit.*

28 From an address by Ben Tillett, *The Dock Labourer's Bitter Cry*, 1889, in Fishman, *op.cit.*

29 Collins, *op.cit.*

30 Collins, *op.cit.*

31 Tom Rollins, 'The disappearing migration routes that brought Aleppo's Jews to Manchester', *Middle East Eye*, 25 May 2016. Lydia Collins, op.cit., points out that the individual in question, Abraham Btesh, 'never put down permanent roots but was a regular visitor for forty years and several of his children settled in Manchester'.

32 Collins, *op.cit.*

33 Julia Maine, *The Jewish community of the south Manchester suburb of Didsbury, 1891-1914: a socio-economic comparison with the Northern sector of the city's Jewry*, assignment for the Open University, updated February 2020, The Jewish Museum, Manchester. https:/ www.webpalette.co.uk/jewishresearch.htm

34 Collins, *op.cit.*

35 https://museumsvictoria.com.au/longform/journeys-to-australia/

36 The real value of this today would be closer to £100.

37 For the details of Nathan's conviction I am grateful to Lesley Abdela, who, in turn, obtained this information from the distinguished historian, Sheila Rowbotham.

38 Sung by followers of the utopian socialist, Robert Owen, on their journey to the New World.

39 Joseph and Rachel Shasha (née Abdela) returned from Buenos Aires after the Second Word War but their son, Eric, stayed on.

40 Lydia Collins, '1917 petition by Baghdad merchants at Manchester', *The Scribe: Journal of Babylonian Jewry*, No.56, January 1993, p.7. The author of this article records that Joseph Abdela was one of the original petitioners.

41 For the early development of Jews in Canada, see Vigod, B.L. (1984) *The Jews in Canada*, Ottawa: Canadian Historical Association.

42 Even before the main influx of Ashkenazi Jews arrived from Poland and Eastern Europe, they formed a community in Montreal. The cornerstone of a new synagogue for the community was laid in 1860 by David Moss, a distant relative who belonged to a family that was active in advancing the welfare of this congregation during three decades. See *Jewish Encyclopaedia*, 1906. http://www jewishencyclopedia.com/articles/14692-victoria

43 Two families who moved to America, the Shashas and a branch of the Abdelas, settled first in New York but some of their offspring moved to other parts of the country.

44 Rosa Luxemburg.

45 Bernstein, E. 'South African Jewish Community', *The American Year Book*, Vol. 73, 1972, pp.580-589.

46 A useful source on the Rothschilds is Johnson, *op.cit.*

47 Zero Mostel, lyric, 'If I were a rich man'.

48 Zangwill, *op.cit.*

49 Nathan, L.D. (1984) *As Old as Auckland: The History of L.D. Nathan and Co. Ltd. and of the David Nathan Family, 1840-1940*, Takapuna, NZ: Benton Ross.

50 This biography, written by Julia Millen, was first published in the *Dictionary of New Zealand Biography* in 1993. I have lightly edited the original version to link it to other sections of this book but I am greatly indebted for access to Julia Millen's excellent portrayal of another member of the Nathan family. Joseph Nathan was in the same lineage as Amelia Nathan, the mother of Moses Joseph (who,

it will be recalled, was the subject of a previous account in this chapter of his business success). Amelia had a brother, Jacob Hyam Nathan, who married Miriam, and the couple, in turn, gave birth to Joseph Nathan's father.

51 Steven Pinker, Canadian scientist and psychologist.

52 David ShaSha, 'Understanding the Sephardi-Ashkenazi split'. https://www.huffpost.com/entry/understanding-the-sephard_b_541033?ir=Australia

53 Extract from James Picciotto (1865), *Sketches of Anglo-Jewish History*, in ShaSha, *op.cit.*

54 Langford, A.M., *op.cit.*, pp.3-20.

55 *Ibid.*

56 David W. Gutzke, 'Improved pubs and road houses: rivals for public affection in interwar England', *The Journal of the Brewery History Society Online*, 119, pp.2-9.

57 Eva Johanna Holmberg, 'Jews of all trades: Jews and their professions in early modern English travel writing', *Journeys*, Vol. 14, Issue 2, pp.27-49.

58 John Cooper, 'How Jews broke into the professions', *The Jewish Chronicle*, 7 November 2012. https://www.thejc.com/comment comment/how-jews-broke-into-the-professions-1.37963

59 *Ibid.*

60 Julia Bess Frank, 'Moses Maomonides: rabbi of medicine', *The Yale Journal of Biology and Medicine*, 54 (1981), pp.79-88.

61 Jerry Muller, in 'Symposium: The Origins of Jewish Creativity', *Moment*, 21 May 2013. https://momentmag.com/symposium-the-origins-of-jewish-creativity/

62 Joshua Fogel, 'Asher Beylin (Beilin)', *Yiddish Lexsikon*. http//ylexsikon.blogspot

63 www.imdb.com

64 Matthew Butson, 'The forgotten ones', *Black and White*, October/November 2001. https://web.archive.org/web/20110814034405/http://corporate.gettyimages.com/masters2/press/articles/BWP_Nahum_Sterling_Baron.pdf

65 Michael Berkowitz, 'A portrait of the unsung visionaries', *The Jewish Chronicle*, 27 April 2016.

66 Genesis 2:18.

67 Judges 4:2-24.

68 Mendel Dubov, 'Why do observant Jews have so many kids?'.

https://www.chabad.org/library/article_cdo/aid/4372320/jewish/
Why-Do-Observant-Jews-Have-So-Many-Kids.htm

69 Meir Soloveichik, 'A Jewish mother: a theology', The Rohr Jewish
Learning Institute. https://www.myjli.com/why/index.
php/2016/11/06/the-jewish-mother-a-theology/

70 Wall slogan in Paris during student and labour unrest, May 1968.

71 Speech to the Conservative Group for Europe, 22 April 1993, urging
the retention of European Union membership.

72 Lesley Abdela, 'Witness to History: A 'boots-on-the-ground' perspective
– fighting for gender balance and gender justice', in *Britain and the
World* 9.1, DOI, Edinburgh: Edinburgh University Press.

73 This is one of a selection of responses in a chapter, 'What women
want', in John Carey (ed.) (1999) *The Faber Book of Utopias*,
London: Faber and Faber.

74 Talmud, in Tractate Baba Bathra.

75 *The Jewish Chronicle*, 27 February 1885.

76 Miriam Steiner, 'Some aspects of Jewish philanthropy in the 19th
century: with special reference to the Manchester Jewish Board
of Guardians'. https://www.jewishgen.org/jcr-uk/Newman_papers/
Provincial_Jewry_Victorian/Philanthropy.htm#top

77 White, J. (2003) *Rothschild Buildings: Life in an East End tenement
block 1887-1920*, London: Pimlico.

78 The Buildings were actually named after Baroness Charlotte de
Rothschild, rather than her son, although it is alleged that on her
death-bed she urged him to devote his efforts to this particular cause.

79 In contrast, external critics condemned the tenement blocks as
dreary and inhumane. Jack London said he would rather step into
the Thames than live in such a place. But this dichotomy between
those who would see it as a step up, and critics viewing it all from a
more abstract stance, is not unusual for new forms of architecture.

80 Zangwill, *op.cit.*

81 *Ibid.*

82 *Ibid.*

83 Suzanne D. Rutland, 'Creating transnational connections:
Australia and California', in Ava F. Kahn, Adam D. Mendelsohn
(eds.) *Transnational Traditions: New Perspectives on American Jewish
History*, (pp.64-83). Detroit: Wayne State University Press.

84 Zangwill, *op.cit.*

85 Erica Jong, in an interview with Whitney Joiner in 2013.

86 Howard Jacobson.

[87] Zangwill, *op.cit.*

[88] Peter Kohn, '180 years of chuppahs', *The Australian Jewish News*, 30 January 2012. https://ajn.timesofisrael.com/180-years-of-chuppahs/

[89] 'The late Mr Moses', *The Sydney Morning Herald*, 22 December 1883.

[90] Jonathan Sacks.

[91] Liam Kay, Third Sector, 29 March 2016. https://www.thirdsector. co.uk/jewish-people-likely-give-charity-rest-population-says-report/ fundraising/article/1389098

[92] John F. Kennedy.

[93] Hanna Nissim, 'Why Jewish giving to Israel is losing ground', *The Conversation*, 15 August 2018. https://theconversation.com/why-jewish-giving-to-israel-is-losing-ground-100946

[94] Josh Nathan-Kazis, '26 billon bucks: the Jewish charity industry uncovered' *Forward*. https://forward.com/news/israel/194978/26-billion-bucks-the-jewish-charity-industry-unco/

[95] Jewish National Fund UK – Supporting Israel for Life. https://www. jnf.co.uk/jnfs-mission-charitable-purposes/

[96] Abrahams, *op.cit.*

[97] Madigan, E. (2019) 'Thou hast given us home and freedom, Mother England: Anglo-Jewish gratitude, patriotism and service during and after the First Word War', in Madigan, E. and Reuveni, G. (eds.) *The Jewish Experience of the First World War*, London: Palgrave Macmillan.

[98] Thomas Macaulay MP, in a speech to the House of Commons (17 April 1833), urging the removal of restrictions on Jews in Britain.

[99] Israel Finestein, 'Anglo-Jewish opinion during the struggle for emancipation, 1828-1858', *Transactions (Jewish Historical Society of England)*, Vol. 20 (1959-61).

[100] 'We were there too', a photographic exhibition of British Jews in the First World War, London Jewish Cultural Centre, 2018. https:// www.jewsfww.uk/home.php

[101] Klein, E. (1996) *Lost Jews: The struggle for identity today*. London: Palgrave Macmillan.

[102] The words of Władysław Szpilman, survivor of the Warsaw Ghetto.

[103] *Ibid.*

[104] 'Jews in Numbers', Board of Deputies of British Jews. https://www. bod.org.uk/jewish-facts-info/jews-in-numbers/

[105] *Ibid.*

[106] Klein, *op.cit.*

[107] William Shakespeare, *The Merchant of Venice* III, i.

[108] Tad Stahnke, William and Sheila Konar Director of International

Educational Outreach, in an interview at the opening of an exhibition, 'Some Were Neighbours', at the UK Holocaust Memorial Museum, 2 February 2020. https://news.un.org/en/tags/anti-semitism

[109] Macaulay, 1833, *op.cit.*

[110] For a concise reference, see 'The Battle of Cable Street', *Encyclopedia Judica.* https://www.jewishvirtuallibrary.org/battle-of-cable-street

[111] Kendal, D. (2008) *Members Only: Elite clubs and the process of exclusion*, Lanham, Maryland: Rowman and Littlefield.

[112] Maimonides, twelfth century.

[113] Encyclopedia Judaica: Hanover, Germany. https://www.jewishvirtuallibrary.org/hanover

[114] *Ibid.*

[115] Colleen Barry, quoting Chief Rabbi Pinchas Goldschmit at an awards ceremony in Rome, in *AP Morning Wire,* 24 October 2019. https://apnews.com/ed35a6487d63436fb07b6460e2626a55

[116] See, for instance, 'A guide to Labour Party anti-Semitism claims', BBC News, 26 June 2020. https://www.bbc.com/news/uk-politics-45030552

[117] The MP in question was Luciana Berger, who accused her party of being institutionally anti-Semitic. She was not the only Jewish member to resign from the party.

[118] This is a non-departmental public body which has responsibility for the promotion and enforcement of equality and non-discrimination laws in England, Scotland and Wales.

[119] Equality and Human Rights Commission, 'Investigation into anti-Semitism in the Labour Party', 20 October 2020.

[120] David Patrikarakos, 'Anti-Semitism and the two sides of Britain', *The Spectator (Coffee House)*, 2 Nov. 2020.

[121] David Cameron, in an interview with Jeffrey Goldberg, in *The Atlantic*, 17 April 2015. https://www.theatlantic.com/international/archive/2015/04/david-cameron-on-anti-zionism-and-anti-semitism/390759/

[122] Midrash Tanhuma, *Kedoshim* 10.

[123] John Milton, *Paradise Regained*.

[124] Joshua 1: 2-4.

[125] Deuteronomy 7: 6 and 14.

[126] Extract from the Balfour Declaration, 1917.

[127] Official Records of the General Assembly, 52nd Meeting, New York: United Nations.

[128] Official Records of the General Assembly, Second Session,

Supplement No. 11, document A/364 Report of the United Nations Special Committee on Palestine, Vol. IV.

[129] *Ibid*, Vol II.

[130] 'This land is your land', lyric, Woody Guthrie.

[131] *Australian Jewish News*, 21 April 2020. https://ajn.timesofisrael.com/global-jewish-population-hits-14-7-million/

[132] I owe a personal debt to Professor Yaacov Oved, a pioneer of Kibbutz Palmachim, who is a foremost scholar of the kibbutz as well as a lifelong practitioner of community living.

[133] David Lowenthal (1985), *The Past is a Foreign Country*, Cambridge, UK: Cambridge.

[134] L.P. Hartley (1953), *The Go-Between*, London: Hamish Hamilton.

Lightning Source UK Ltd.
Milton Keynes UK
UKHW021344250522
403506UK00008B/1075